Man's Rights

Or

How Would You Like it?

Comprising Dreams.

Annie Denton Cridge

First publication: 1870, William Denton, Boston

"Holding the mirror up to Nature."

"Oh, wad some power the giftie gie us,

To see oursels as ithers see us!"

"It was MY *cow that was gored by* YOUR *ox."*

Contents

Dream Number One.

LAST night I had a dream, which may have a meaning.

I stood on a high hill that overlooked a large city. The proud spires of many churches rose high, here and there; and round about the city were beautiful, sloping hills, stretching away, away into the distance; while a broad river wound here and there, extending a kindly arm toward the city.

As I stood there, wondering what manner of city it was, its name, and the character of its inhabitants, all at once I found myself in its very midst. From house to house I flitted; from kitchen to kitchen; and lo! everywhere the respective duties of man and woman were reversed; for in every household I found the men in aprons, superintending the affairs of the kitchen. Everywhere men, and only men, were the Bridgets and housekeepers. I thought that those gentlemen-housekeepers looked very pale, and somewhat nervous; and, when I looked into their spirits (for it seemed in my dream that I had the power), I saw anxiety and unrest, a constant feeling of unpleasant expectancy, – the result of a long and weary battling with the cares of the household.

As I looked at those men-Bridgets and gentleman-housekeepers, I said to myself, "This is very strange! Why, these men seem unsexed! How stoop-shouldered they are! how weak and complaining their voices."

I found, too, that not only was the kitchen exclusively man's, but also the nursery: in fact, all the housework was directed and done by men. I felt a sad pity for these men, as I flitted from house to house, from kitchen to kitchen, from nursery to nursery.

I saw them in the houses of the poor, where the "man did his own work." I saw him in the morning arise early, light the fire, and begin to prepare the breakfast, his face pale and haggard. "No wonder!" I thought, when I saw how he hurried, hurried, while in his spirit was a constant fear that the baby would awake. Very soon I heard the sharp cry of the baby; and away ran the poor father, soon returning with baby in his arms, carrying it around with him, while he raked the fire, fried the meat, and set the table for breakfast. When all was ready, down came two or three unwashed, unkempt children, who must be attended to: and, when all this was done, I observed that the poor gentleman's appetite was gone; and, pale and nervous, he sat down in the rocking-chair, with the baby in his arms. But what greatly astonished me was to see how quietly and composedly the lady of the house drank her coffee and read the morning paper; apparently oblivious of the trials of her poor husband, and of all he had to endure in connection with his household cares.

It was wash-day, and I watched him through that long and weary day. First at the wash-tub, while baby slept; then rocking the cradle and washing at the same time; then preparing dinner, running and hurrying here and there about the house: while in his poor, disturbed mind revolved the thought of the sewing that ought to be done, and only his own hands to do it.

Evening came, and the lady of the house returned to dinner. The children came to meet her; and as she lifted up one, and then another, and kissed them, I thought! "Why, how beautiful is that woman!" Then in my dream I seemed to behold every woman of that strange city; and ah! the marvellous beauty of those women! Eye hath not seen, neither hath it entered into the heart of man to conceive; for a beauty almost angelic was so charmingly combined with intellect, and health brooded so divinely over all, that, at the *tout ensemble*, I was profoundly astonished and intensely delighted.

Then I turned myself about, and was again in the home I had left. It was evening: the lamp on the table was lighted, and there sat the poor husband I have described, in his rocking-chair, darning stockings and mending the children's clothes after the hard day's washing. I saw that it had rained; that the clothes-line had broken, and dropped the clothes in the dirty yard; and the poor man had had a terrible time rinsing some and washing others over again; and that he had finally put them down in wash-tubs, and covered them with water he had brought from a square distant. But the day's work was over; and there he moved to and fro, while his wife, in comfortable slippers, sat by the fire reading.

"Well," I said to myself, "such is the home of the lowly; but how is it where one or more servants can be kept?" Then, as by magic, I saw how it was; for I found myself in a kitchen where a male Bridget was at work, his hair uncombed, his face and hands unwashed, and his clothes torn and soiled. Bridget was cooking breakfast, a knife in his hand, while he was bending over the cooking-stove, moodily talking to himself. The gentleman-housekeeper, pale and unhappy, opened the door, looked at Bridget, but said nothing, and soon went into the dining-room. As soon as his back was turned, Bridget turned around, lifted the arm that held the knife, and, with a fiendish look, whispered to himself, "I would like to strike you with this."

Breakfast on the table, I looked, and beheld bad coffee, burned meat, and heavy biscuits; and I heard the lady of the house, who sat in a morning-robe and spangled slippers, say to the poor gentleman, —

"My dear, this breakfast is bad, very bad: you ought to attend to things better."

I observed how sad he felt at these words; and I did pity the poor fellow. It seemed to me that I staid a whole day with this poor gentleman. His health was very feeble: he was suffering from dyspepsia. I saw him attending the children, saw him sewing, saw him go nervously into the kitchen, and sadly and wearily attend to things there, while the dark glances of the male Bridget followed him viciously everywhere. I saw the waste and thieving of that man-Bridget, and saw how completely that poor gentleman felt crushed and held by his help. My heart yearned toward that poor, feeble housekeeper, unable to do his own work, and so much at the mercy of that terrible Bridget; and I ceased to wonder at the pale faces of the men everywhere.

The homes of the wealthy I visited; and almost everywhere I found those gentleman-housekeepers anxious and worried, no matter how many servants were kept. There was trouble about washing, trouble about ironing, trouble about children: there was waste, there was thieving; and, oh! the number of poor, sickly gentlemen I found made me very sad.

And while, in my dream, my heart was going out in pity and commiseration toward those gentlemen-housekeepers, I found myself in the midst of a large assembly, composed exclusively of these men. Here almost every man in the city had congregated to hold an indignation-meeting, — a housekeeper's indignation-meeting. Every man wore a white kitchen-apron, and some I noticed whose sleeves were white with flour, while others had pieces of dough here and there stuck on their clothes: others, again, had hanging on their arms dish-cloths and towels. Very many, too, had babies in their arms, and one or more children at their side.

Then I listened to some of their speeches. One gentleman said, —

"I have kept house sixteen years; and I know what it is to be poor and do my own work; and I know what it is to have servants: and I tell you, gentlemen, the whole system of housekeeping, as now conducted, is a bad one. It is, in the first place, wasteful and extravagant; and, in the next place, it wears out our bodies and souls. See how pale and feeble we are! It is time there was a change."

"We don't each of us make our own shoes," said another speaker; "we don't each of us spin our own yarn, or weave our own cloth: the hand-loom has departed, and it is now done by machinery, which has so far come to our rescue. It is not so bad for us as for our grandfathers, who had to weave on a hand-loom all the muslin and cloth for the family; but it is bad enough. Here we are kept every day of our lives over the cook-stove, wash-tub, or ironing-table, or thinking about them. Can nothing be done to remedy this? Can not all the domestic work be done by machinery? Can not it be done on wholesale principles? I say it can: there is no more need for a kitchen to any house than for a spindle or a loom."

Then followed many more speeches about the extravagance of the present system, whereby one or two persons, and often more, were employed in doing the work of a small family, when it might be done at much less expense for one-fourth the labor, were the wholesale principle applied to that as it is to other things.

One man remarked that the kitchen was a small retail shop to every house: another called it a dirt-producing establishment for every family, sending its fumes and filth to every room. Another gentleman said that the fine pictures painted about the domestic hearth, happy homes, &c., were all moonshine, and would continue so just as long as the present state of things continued.

"I protest against the present state of things," said a tall, delicate man, with a large, active brain. "We have this matter in our own hands; and let us here and now begin something practical. Instead of forty little extravagant cooking-stoves, with each a Bridget, and so many gentlemen employed as housekeepers, let us have one large stove, and do our cooking, washing, and ironing on a large scale."

Well, I thought in my dream that I listened to hundreds of speeches and protests and denunciations.

Then the scene changed; and forthwith there sprang up large cooking-establishments in different parts of the city, that could, as if by magic, supply hundreds of families with their regular meals. I looked, and lo! what machinery had done in the weaving of cloth, above and beyond what had been effected by the hand-loom, was accomplished here. The inventive genius of the age had been at work; and the result was a wondrous machine that could cook, wash, and iron for hundreds of people at once.

"I must see the workings of that establishment," I said in my dream; and forthwith a polite gentleman, who said that he had been a housekeeper twenty-five years, and knew all the petty annoyances of the old system, kindly proposed to show me the various doings of the machinery.

"We are going to cook dinner now," he said, as he walked toward a monster machine. He touched a handle, and then about fifty bushels of potatoes were quietly let down into a large cistern, where they were washed, and then moved forward into a machine for peeling; which operation was accomplished in a minute or two by its hundreds of knives, and the potatoes came out all ready to be cooked. Turnips went through the same process, and other vegetables were prepared and made ready for the huge cooking apparatus. All was done by machinery: there was no lifting, no hauling, no confusion; but the machines, like things of life, lifted, prepared, and transferred as desired.

I saw what was called a "self-feeding pie-maker," that reminded me of a steam printing-press, where the paper goes in blank at one end and comes out printed at the other. So the flour, shortening, and fruit were taken in all at once at three separate receptacles, and came out at the other end pies ready for the oven, to which they were at once, over a small tramway, transferred by machinery. Another machine made cakes and pies.

Meal-time came: the dinner was to be served. Two large wooden doors opened by means of a spring which the gentleman touched with his foot. Through them came filing past us, one after another, small, curiously constructed steam-wagons, the motion of which caused but little noise, as the wheels were tired with vulcanized India-rubber: those wagons were so arranged as to travel on common roads, and much resembled caravans. They moved past machines which were called "servers," where meals were dished and transferred to the steam caravans, which latter were termed "waiters." All this was done systematically, quietly, yet rapidly, by a few persons in charge of the machines by which meals were prepared for and distributed to hundreds of families. I saw that there were hundreds of these "servers," as well as hundreds of waiters; so that the dinner was dished and served almost simultaneously, in double-tin cases, containing all requisites for the table.

Then away went the steam "waiters," delivering the meals almost simultaneously at the houses, which, by the by, were rapidly being "reconstructed" to meet the new state of things, with dining-rooms to accommodate hundreds at once, in blocks, or hollow squares, with cook-houses, laundries, &c., at the center, or in circles similarly arranged, combining, in a most inconceivable degree, economy with beauty.

To return to the steam waiters: At a time understood, they called for the tin cases containing dishes and *débris*, and then wended their way back to headquarters, where all the dishes were washed and transferred to their places by steam-power.

The washing and ironing, I discovered, was done in the same expeditious manner, by machinery; several hundred pieces going in at one part of the machine dirty, and coming out at the other end a few minutes afterward, rinsed and ready to dry. The ironing was as rapid as it was perfect, – smooth, glossy, uncreased, unspecked; all done by machinery.

Then I looked once more into this strange city, and, behold! an emancipated class! The pale, sickly faces of the men were giving place to ruddy health. Anxiety, once so marked in their features, was departing. No Bridget to dread now; no washing-day any more; no sad faces nor neglected children: for now the poor gentlemen-housekeepers had time to attend to the children, and to the cultivation of their own minds; and I saw that the dream of the poet and of the seer was realized: for husband and wife sat side by side, each sharing the joys of the other. Science and philosophy, home and children, were cemented together; for peace, sweet peace, had descended like a dove on every household.

I awoke: it was all a dream. My husband stood at my bedside. "Annie, Annie!" he said: "awake, Annie! that new girl of yours is good for nothing. You will have to rise and attend to her, else I shall have no breakfast. I have been late at the office for several days past, and I fear I shall be late again."

I arose: and, as my husband ate his breakfast, I pondered over my strange dream. As soon as he was gone, I transferred it to paper, feeling that it really did mean something, and is intended as a prophecy of the "good time coming," when women will be rid of the kitchen and cook-stove, and the possibilities of the age actualize for woman that which I have dreamed for man.

Dream Number Two.

ONCE again I have visited that strange city in dream-land, where men, and only men, were the housekeepers and Bridgets.

It is midnight: I have just awakened from my dream, and risen to pen it down, lest in the morning I should find my memory treacherous. My good husband has protested against writing by gas-light, and very gravely given his opinion on midnight writing; and – ah, well! he is sound asleep now, I see; and so at once to my dream.

I thought my husband and I were walking along some beautiful streets, when all at once I exclaimed, "Why, husband! here we are together in that very city I told you about, where the men are the housekeepers and kitchen-girls. Oh, I'm glad! Let us find out every thing about these inhabitants, both men and women."

While we were talking together, several gentlemen, pale and delicate in appearance, passed us. Some were dressed in calico suits, trimmed with little ruffles – ruffles round the bottom of the pants, ruffles down the front and round the tails of the coats; and on both sides of the button-holes of their vests were rows of small ruffles. From some of their little flat hats flowed ribbon-streamers; while on others were placed, jauntily and conspicuously, feathers and flowers.

More and more gentlemen passed us. What a variety of costume! I was almost bewildered; gentlemen in red, green, yellow, drab, and black suits, trimmed in such elaborate and fanciful styles! Some suits were parti-colored; that is to say, the pants perhaps yellow or red, the vest blue, the coat green, crimson, or drab. Some of these suits were trimmed with lace: lace down the sides of the pants and round the bottoms; lace round the edges of the coat, and beautifully curving hither and thither as a vine, over the backs and down the fronts of the coats; and also over the fronts of the vests. Some suits were almost covered with elaborate embroidery, or satin folds, or piping, or ribbon, while bows and streamers of the same or contrasting colors, according to taste, were placed on the backs of the coats, shoulders, and, here and there, on the vest and pants. It really makes me laugh at this moment to think of that comical sight. Their head-dresses, too, were most fantastic; flowers, bits of lace, tulle or blonde, feathers, and even birds, were mixed in endless profusion with ribbon, tinsel, glitter, and (*ad libitum*) grease. Many of these gentlemen carried little portemonnaies, which hung on their jewelled fingers by tiny chains. Others carried fans, some edged with feathers, or covered with pictures, or inlaid with pearl, &c., varying, I supposed, according to the purse.

Each of these gentlemen seemed particularly interested in every other gentleman's costume; for they turned and looked at each other, while several exclamations reached my ear; such as, "What a superb suit!" "What a splendid coat!" "What a darling vest!" "What a love of a hat!"

These gentlemen had a swinging gate, something like that of a sailor, that made their coat-tails move to and fro as they walked. I noticed, too, that they were very careful of their pants, which were decidedly wide; for on passing over a gutter or soiled part of the pavement, they carefully and daintily raised the legs of the pants with the finger and thumb. This impressed me favorably as to their love of cleanliness; for otherwise the laces, ribbons, embroidery, or ruffles which graced the bottoms of their pants, would have come in contact with the mud of the streets.

As we stood looking at those strange gentlemen, my husband suggested the idea of a masquerade. Then suddenly I found myself alone, and flitting from dwelling to dwelling, from home to home; and everywhere the gentlemen were dressed in flimsy materials, and all more or less decked with trimmings.

I found the majority of gentlemen busy with needlework, some doing the sewing of the family; but many, very many, with their sons, dressed in delicate morning suits, doing fancy-work. Some were working little cats and dogs on footstools; others were busy with embroidery, fancy knitting, and all the delicate nothings that interest only ladies in this waking world of ours.

As I listened to their conversation, which was generally composed of gossip, fashion, or love-matters, – for the male sex took the fashion-books, and not ladies, and these I found in the majority of homes, headed "Gentlemen's Magazine of Fashions," – as I listened to their conversation, I repeat, and observed all this, my soul was filled with unutterable sadness. "Alas! alas!" I said: "what means this degradation? Why have the lords of creation become mere puppets or dolls? Where is the loftiness and intellectuality of *man – noble man!*"

Just then I was aroused from my reverie by an aspiring young gentleman who was sewing some ruffles on the legs of his pants, saying to his father, "I don't see, papa, why men can not earn money as well as women: I want to learn a business."

"That is all nonsense," replied his father: "your business is to get married. There is no necessity for a *boy* to learn a *business;* what you have to do is to learn to be a good housekeeper; for you will be married some day, and will have to attend to your children and your wife; and that is enough business for any man."

"But I may not marry," said the boy; "and I know I will not, unless I can get a woman with money, that can give me a good home."

Then they talked about Mr. Some-one – I could not catch the name – that had married well: his wife was worth over fifty thousand dollars, and was very kind to him, taking him to theaters and concerts, and wherever he wanted to go: she let him, too, have all the dress he wanted. She had only one fault: she would not allow him to go anywhere unless she accompanied him.

Oh! my soul was sick with sympathy and pity for that race of poor degraded men! "What does it mean?" I asked myself: "why are they in this pitiable condition?"

Then, for the first time, I realized that this city was the capital of a great nation; that women, and only women, were the lawmakers, judges, executive officers, &c., of the nation; that every office of honor and emolument was filled by women; that all colleges and literary institutions, with very few exceptions, were all built for women, and only open to women, and that men were all excluded. I went from school to school, from college to college; and, ah! the beauty, the dignity, of those women! Science and art had truly crowned them with their own best gifts: their faces seemed to me almost divine; and, ah! what a contrast to the vain, silly, half-educated men who staid at home, or paraded the streets, thinking principally of fashion and dress! for these women were everywhere dressed in plain, substantial clothing, which lent them such a charm that I realized instinctively there was something about them far more beautiful than beauty.

As I looked upon these women in the colleges, as students and professors, as lawyers, judges, and jurors, as I looked upon them in the lecture-room and the pulpit, the house of representatives and the senate-chamber, – yea, everywhere, – I observed their quiet dignity, clothed in their plain flowing robes; and I was almost tempted to believe that Nature had intended – in this part of the world at least – that woman, and only woman, should legislate and govern; and that here, if nowhere else, woman should be superior to man.

In the galleries of the legislative bodies were hundreds of gentlemen, young and old, looking on, and listening to the speeches made by the lady members. How they fluttered and fanned and whispered and smiled!

"Alas, for fallen man!" I said. Then, in an instant, I had, as by one glance, looked into the pockets of every lady and gentleman present, and also into the acquisitive pockets of the brain of each; and the result proved to me, that, as man held the purse with us, so woman held the purse in that wonderful dream-land. To obtain money from their wives, those weak, silly men would often resort to cajolery and deceit. Only from their wives could they obtain money for dress or any thing else; and so, as by common consent, nearly all the husbands had seemingly decided that they had a right to get all they could out of their wives, without any reference to the question whether the wife could afford it or not. Thus I found, that the woman being the purse-holder, she the giver and he the receiver, worked most disastrously; for it made the interests of wife and husband separate: the interest of the wife was not the interest of the husband, his greatest care being to get all he could, and spend all he could get.

I left those buildings, and took the street-cars. Here those noble-looking, stately women escorted the gentlemen to the cars, stood while the gentlemen walked in first, then demurely stepped on board, and paid the car-fare for both. What impressed me as much as any thing I saw was, with what matter-of-course style the gentlemen, in their dainty, flimsy, flying garments, occupied the seats of the cars, while the ladies stood; or, if a lady had a seat, with what noble demeanor she rose and gave it up if a gentlemen stepped on board. I saw that those ladies took gentlemen to theaters and places of amusement; ladies took those gentlemen to church, and very kindly saw them safely home; ladies told those gentlemen how beautiful they looked, how prettily they were dressed, &c.; and I saw that it gave these poor, weak-minded men much pleasure.

In ice-cream saloons and other places of refreshment, these gentlemen were as kindly and as gallantly taken by the ladies, who, in all cases, paid for the refreshments.

I looked into the churches, which were principally filled with elegantly-dressed gentlemen. "Ah!" I said to myself, "in religion these down-trodden men find some consolation;" but, in an instant, I was shocked by realizing that more than half went from custom, or to show their dress and see the fashions.

I looked into the prayer-meetings, and (being, of course, all the time invisible) was also present at the confessionals; and in both, the excess of men who attended was a remarkable fact.

Men got up sewing-societies and mite-societies; and, in these, many sad, sorrowful men found a few moments, sometimes, of happy, useful existence.

Occasionally, in those public places I found a man who had risen above his fellows, who had become famous in literature. I met with some male poets, and several conversant with science in a degree equal to the best of women. And I said to myself," If these *few* men have proved themselves equal to the best of women, then is it not strong presumptive evidence that *all* these men would be equal to women, were they equally educated?"

Then I seemed in my dream to grasp the *cause* of all this difference between the sexes; and that these beautiful, noble women might have been in the same deplorable condition had they been trained and educated as these degraded men, – without a motive in life, limited in education and culture, shut out of every path to honor or emolument, and reduced to the condition of paupers on the bounty of the opposite sex. I saw that the disadvantages under which one sex thus labored constituted a curse that extended to both; and that, though the drudgery of the kitchen had been removed, it was not the millennium, by any means, as I had supposed in my last dream, but only the beginning of the millennium. Man was not the only sufferer, but the wrong due to man acted and re-acted on woman; for men, being defrauded in their education, and nearly all avenues to pecuniary independence closed to them, marriage, with those half-educated, dependent creatures called men, was necessarily their highest ambition. There was no other way for them to obtain wealth or a home; hence they devoted all their powers to the one grand object of catching a woman with money; hence woman became also the sufferer, being often trapped into marriage by one of these silly, worthless men, who had learned well the arts and schemes of wife-catching.

I looked into the thought-cells of these ladies' brains, and found stored therein, in almost every instance, a decided belief that men constituted the inferior, and women the superior sex.

There is a bright side, however, to every picture; and even my dream had its bright side. For instance: I had dreamed that I looked in on the gentlemen with pale face and haggard countenance, of whom I spoke in my first dream as a man that "did his own work;" and now, instead of toil and anxiety about meals, washing, ironing, &c., he was in the garden with his children, planting vegetable-seeds and flower-seeds; and as I with pleasure noted his returning health and strength, I listened to his talk with the children, whom he was interesting with a story.

How I lingered with that gentleman! I accompanied him to the house, and saw him reading; I looked over his book, and was delighted to find that he was studying physiology. By and by he began to talk with the children about the nerves, which he called electric wires carrying messages to the brain; which delighted the children: and I said in deep reverence, "Thank God, that man has been emancipated from the kitchen! he will work out his own salvation: the golden key of the universe has he grasped with his own right hand, and it will open to him every door in the arcana of Nature. Not for ever will man be considered woman's inferior."

Then, like a flash, came to me the mental and moral status of every man in that great country; and I realized that with emancipation from the kitchen had come a hungering and thirsting for education, for mental aliment.

Then I turned; and, lo! I stood in the street, where great posters caught my eye: —

"MAN'S RIGHTS!
A Lecture on Man's Rights,"

I read.

Fain would I have attended a lecture on man's rights; but, in my eagerness to do so, I awoke.

P.S. — It is morning; and, to my great joy, I have had another dream. As I retired to my bed after writing the above, instantly Dreamland was present, and the thread taken up where it was dropped. I have attended lectures on *Man's Rights,* and Man's Rights Conventions; all of which I must write down at once, even if my husband has to go without his breakfast; for dreams so often take to themselves wings and fly away!

Dream Number Three.

WHO can divine the philosophy of dreams? Who can account for the fact that persons visit again and again places they have never beheld by physical eyes, and talk with people they have only known in Dreamland? How real become to us the places and the people we have repeatedly visited in our dreams! Who have not experienced something of this reality in their own dreaming?

But it does seem especially remarkable to me, that, after having penned down at midnight one dream, I should, on returning to my pillow, have found myself in the very spot where my late dream ended; again in that strange city, again looking at the large posters headed, –

"MAN'S RIGHTS!!
Mr. Sammie Smiley, Mr. Johnnie Smith, and Others,
Will address the meeting on the
Rights of Man!"

I was pleased on coming to these words: "Discussion is invited." "I will go," I said, and turned to follow the crowd; but, as by magic, was transferred to one of the large cooking-establishments which I saw in my first dream, and soon recognized it to be the same.

There were the huge machines at work cooking dinner, while in a comfortable rocking-chair sat the same gentleman who had in that same dream showed me over the establishment. He was reading a newspaper. "Ah!" he said, as he looked up from his paper, "glad to see you, madam. You see I have time to read while the dinner is cooking. All goes on well. We supply one-eighth of the city with meals, and everybody is satisfied, nay, more than satisfied: they are delighted with the arrangement; for every poor man is relieved of washing, ironing, and cooking. And yet all this is done at less cost than when every house had its little selfish, dirty kitchen."

"And what is this about 'man's rights'?" I asked. "I see posters all over your city, headed, 'Man's Rights!'"

He smiled as he replied, "Well, madam, emancipating man from the drudgery of the kitchen has given him leisure for thought; and, in his thinking, he had discovered that he labors under many wrongs, and is deprived of quite as many rights. The idea of men lecturing, men voting, men holding office, &c., excites considerable ridicule; but ridicule proves nothing."

"Are you going to the lecture?" I asked.

"I will go if I have company," he replied; "but it would not look well for me to go alone: besides, I would be afraid to go home so late."

I made no answer; but I thought musingly, "Afraid! afraid of what? of what can these men be afraid? I wonder if there are any wild beasts prowling around this strange city at night. Perhaps there are wolves or mad dogs; but then he is a man, and could carry a revolver and protect himself." But, as by a flash, the truth came to me, and I wondered I had not thought of it before. In this land, *woman* is the natural protector; and so, of course, he was afraid to go without a lady to take care of him.

I had scarcely arrived at this conclusion, when I found myself *en rapport* with every husband in that city. "I would like to go to the lecture on 'men's rights,'" I heard one man say to his wife very timidly.

"I shall go to no such place," replied his wife loftily; "neither will you. 'Man's rights,' indeed!"

"Let us go to the lecture," said another husband to his wife, with a pleasant smile on his face.

"No, no, my dear," replied the lady: "I like you just as you are; and I don't admire womanish men. Nothing is more disgusting than feminine men. We don't want men running to the polls, and electioneering: what would become of the babies at such times?"

Then I looked in on a bevy of young boys ranging in age from sixteen to twenty. How they did laugh at the very mention of "man's rights," as they put on their pretty coats and hats, looking in the mirror, and turning half round to see how their coat-tails looked!

"Man's rights!" said one. "I have all the rights I want."

"So have I," said a young boy of nineteen. "I don't want any more rights."

"We'll have rights enough, I presume, when we get married," said a tall boy of seventeen, as he touched up the flowers in his pretty hat, and perched it carefully on his head.

"Are you all ready?" said a lady, looking into the room. "Come, I want you all to learn your rights to-night. I warrant that after to-night you will want to carry the purse, don the long robes, and send us ladies into the nursery to take care of the babies!"

Hundreds of ladies and gentlemen were on their way to the meeting; and it rejoiced me greatly to find in the hearts of many of the ladies a profound respect for the rights of man, and a sincere desire that man should enjoy every right equally with themselves.

Then I found myself in the lecture-room, which was well filled with ladies and gentlemen, many of whom seemed greatly amused as they whispered and smiled to each other. Very soon three little gentlemen and one rather tall, thin, pale-faced gentlemen walked to the platform, and were received with great demonstrations of applause and suppressed laughter. The audience were evidently not accustomed to hear *gentlemen* lecture.

"How ridiculous those men look!" I heard one elderly lady say. "What does it look like to see a parcel of men pretending to make speeches, in their tawdry pants and fly-away coat-tails, covered with finery and furbelows?"

"They sadly lack the dignity," said another female, "that belongs to ladies and long robes."

"They are decidedly out of their sphere," I heard another remark.

The meeting was opened by the tall gentleman being nominated as president, who at once introduced Mr. Sammie Smiley to the audience, remarking that Mr. Sammie Smiley, with whom they were probably all acquainted by reputation, would address the audience on the all-important subject of *Man's Rights.*

"*Sammie Smiley!*" said a young lady contemptuously. "Suppose we should call ourselves *Lizzie* instead of Elizabeth, or *Maggie* instead of Margaret. Their very names lack dignity."

Mr. Sammie Smiley stepped to the front of the platform with remarkable self-possession for one of the gentlemen of that Dreamland. He wore a suit of black silk, – coat, vest, and pants all alike, bordered with broad black lace. He wore no ornaments, except ear-rings, a plain breastpin, and one or two rings on the fingers. Very good taste, I thought.

"Ladies and gentlemen," he said, "our subject this evening is the *Rights of Man;* but to properly understand this question, it would be well, before considering man's *rights,* to define his *wrongs.*"

"Hear, hear!" applauded the audience.

"Education," he continued, "commences with childhood; and men's wrongs also commence with childhood, inasmuch as they are restricted from healthful physical exercise. The merry, active boy, that would romp and play like his sister, is told that it would be improper for a boy. How often your little son has to be reminded that a *boy* must not do so and so: he must be a dear little gentleman, and not rough and boisterous like a girl.

"He is kept in over-heated rooms; seldom breathes the pure air of heaven; and when he is taken out, how different his dress from that of the girl! Look at his flimsy pants of white muslin; look at his flimsy jacket and paper shoes: and contrast them with the warm cloth dress, the substantial over-garments, and thick shoes of the girl! Think how seldom the boy is permitted to inhale the life-giving, open atmosphere! The girl may romp and play in the snow, climb fences and trees, and thus strengthen every muscle; while the little pale-faced boy presses his nose against the window-pane, and wishes – alas! vainly – that he, too, had been a girl.

"The course of training for our boys causes weakness and disease in after-life, and more than a natural degree of muscular inferiority. The pale faces of boys are a sad contrast to the rosy-cheeked girls in the same family. In our boys is laid, not by Nature, but by ignorance and custom, the foundation for bodily weakness, consequently dependence and mental imbecility: in our girls, muscular strength and their accompaniments, independence and vivacity, both of body and mind. Were boys subject to the same physical training as girls (and no valid reason can be given why they should not be), the result would prove that no natural inferiority exists.

"True education I conceive to be the harmonious development of the whole being, both physical and mental. The natural or physical is before the intellectual. First the stalk, then the ear, and then the full corn in the ear. Through ignorance of these primary truths, many well-intentioned fathers hurry their children to premature graves.

"Why is it that, of all the children born, one-fifth die annually? Can not this large mortality be traced to the present ignorance of *males?* Can it not be traced to their flimsy and imperfect educational training? If men had their rights, were all literary institutions as free to one sex as to the other, our young men would be taught what is of the utmost importance for them to know, but what is kept sedulously from them; viz., a knowledge of mental and physical science.

"Let man be educated as liberally as woman; let him be made to feel the value of a sound mind, and that the brightest ornament to man, as well as woman, is intellect: then, and not until then, will he stand forth in all his beauty.

"We frequently hear that woman's mind is superior to man's; and therefore he ought not to have equal educational facilities. If, as is stated by the opponents of man's rights, men are naturally and necessarily inferior to women, it must follow that they should have superior opportunities for mental culture. If, on the other hand, men are by nature mentally equal to women, no reason can be given why they should not have equal educational facilities."

In the midst of the audience, a beautiful, stately woman rose, and said, that, if it was not out of order, she would like to ask a question: Did not the literature written expressly for men – gentlemen's magazines, gentlemen's fashion-books, &c., – prove their inferiority? This question caused a laugh, and round after round of applause; but the little gentleman-speaker smilingly replied, that many gentlemen never read the trash prepared for them just as simple reading is prepared for children: but the works written for *women* to read, they study and digest, feeling that they were as much for them as for women. The lecturer then continued by stating the appreciative estimates of the truth of science and philosophy evinced by men as well as women, which would be the case to a still greater extent as the *opportunities* for culture were increased, when gentlemen's books and their flimsy trash would disappear; that even were man weaker in judgment than woman, it did not follow that he should never use it; and, if women did all the reasoning for man, it would not be surprising if he had lost the power to reason.

"Pretty good, Mr. Sammie Smiley," said a lady near me.

"Smiley can reason pretty well: that is pretty good logic," remarked another. Then applause after applause rose, accompanied by stamping and clapping of hands, while some young folks in the back of the hall crowed like roosters.

It was really very funny; but Mr. Sammie Smiley took no notice of the proceeding. He referred to the exclusion of men from nearly all occupations, from governing States to measuring tape; also that men were paid only one-third of the wages of women, even for the same work, their occupations being mainly restricted to sewing and teaching; while women could do both these, and whatever else they chose. He urged the gentlemen to push their way into the employment and professions of women, and be equal sharers in the rights of humanity.

Mr. Johnnie Smith then made an excellent speech on man's civil and political rights; but the discussion that followed so interested me that I can not at this moment recall it. When he sat down, a lady arose, and said, that, as discussions were allowed, she desired to make a few remarks.

"Take the platform! take the platform!" said several voices, which she accordingly did.

"What ease! what dignity!" said I mentally, as she stood there in her long, flowing robes. "Ah, woman! thou art verily transfigured."

Then I looked around on that audience, and am compelled to say that the comparison between the sexes was any thing but flattery to the gentlemen. Woman as I am, I love above all things to behold the beautiful face of a woman; but here was womanly beauty exceeding our highest conceptions; and in profound reverence I said, "Our Father in heaven, I thank thee for human beauty. Teach us the laws of beauty, that we, thy children, may people this earth with beautiful beings. Homeliness is akin to ignorance and sin; while beauty of form and beauty of intellect constitute God's best gifts to mortals.

"Those two gentlemen," said the lady, "have given us many good things to-night. There are very few persons who do not know that our sons and husbands ought to be better educated and better paid for their labor; but shall we, for this reason, make them presidents and senators? How would they look in the senate-chamber in their style of dress, so lacking in dignity? Why, we should have them quarreling and pulling hair very soon!"

"Ha, ha!" laughed the audience.

"No, no, gentlemen! you can discuss fashion and money-spending far better than national affairs. Besides, what would become of the babies? Do you propose that we, the women, shall take these your duties upon us? Depend upon it you are wrong, gentlemen: the sphere of man is *home;* and I am decidedly opposed to taking man out of his sphere. Let us for a moment see what Nature teaches on this subject; let us look at man divested of his embroidery and trimming; look at his angular, long form; look at his hairy face. Is he not in his outward structure and appearance more allied to the lower animals? Look at him, and do you not at once think of the monkey? [Hear, hear!] Now turn to woman. Look at her! Does not Nature delight in curves as in lines of beauty?

"See how the planets as they revolve in their orbits delight in curves? It is Nature's perfect method of form and motion. Now look at woman's beautifully curved face and bust, and compare her form in its curved outlines with the angular outlines of man's form, and tell me if Nature herself has not put the stamp of inferiority on man! Ah, woman's face is enough! No mask of hair does she wear; but clear as the sun and fair as the moon shines clearly every feature, thus conclusively attesting her superiority. Again: how well Nature knows the superiority of woman and the inferiority of man, inasmuch as she has chosen women for maternity. Ah! Nature knew where to find the perfect mould for her handiwork; Nature knew which is the superior sex: –

"'Very near to the infinite nature,
Very near to the hand of God,
More rich than the hills of Beulah,
Which the white feet of angels trod,
Is the sacred heart of woman;

The nature by which alone
The divine can become embodied,
And the spirit reach its home.'

"Let us look at this matter from another stand-point. Nature is harmonious in all her parts. If, as I have proved, woman is physically superior, then she is mentally superior; and as man is physically inferior, so, as he must be harmonious in all his parts, he is necessarily and unmistakably inferior in all other respects."

I thought in my dream that I was greatly dissatisfied with the lady's speech, and I did pity the little gentlemen on the platform who were forced to hear so much about their inferiority.

"One more argument," said the lady, "and I am done; and this argument is also drawn from Nature. Woman has phrenologically a larger organ of language than man. Now, what does this teach us? It teaches us this (and it ought to teach every man the same truth): *that woman is the natural orator;* that it is she who should be the lecturer, the speech-maker, the orator, and not man. It teaches us that women as senators and representatives, as lecturers and orators, are where they belong, where Nature intended they should be. It teaches us more than this: that, as man has smaller language than woman, his sphere is the domestic; is the quiet, the silent, the unobtrusive; is one of *silent* influences, not public and demonstrative like that of woman."

She sat down, and I was really glad. "Woman superior to man!" I exclaimed to myself. "Well, some people can prove any thing. I do hope that little gentleman will demolish their sophistry." But, just as Mr. Sammie Smiley arose to reply, I awoke; and, behold! it was all a dream; and I gladly realized, that, in this waking world of ours, man is not considered the inferior of woman, neither is he deprived of his just rights; and I wish sincerely that I could transfer our men to their Dreamland, and that there, at least, in God's universe, there might be one spot where men and women could stand side by side as equals.

Dream Number Four.

IT is said that much dreaming is the result of much eating late at night. However this may accord with the experience of others, very confident am I that *my* dreaming is not thus caused.

When quite a child, I used to visit, in my dreams, a mountain region in which some excavations were going on; but, being there only at night, I never saw any one at work. An old man leaning on a staff, however, invariably met me, and would show me the progress made since a previous visit. Sometimes he would walk with me up a mountain, then down into a valley, where he had a rough log-cabin. This region of Dreamland has been visited by me hundreds of times in my sleep, all those years from childhood to the present time. I meet the same old gentleman, take walks with him in various parts of this same mountain, converse with him on the progress of the excavation, improvements made, &c.

But now to my fourth dream of that strange land where women are considered superior to men.

I dreamed: and, lo! I stood in the same hall where I had attended the meeting on "Man's Rights;" but every seat was vacant. Then I heard the murmur of voices; and, very soon, people began to pour into the hall. Into the minds of those people I had the power to look; and in nearly all was a profound belief in the *rights of men.* Then I turned me about, and looked; and, lo! the capacious hall was filled to overflowing. Several ladies and gentlemen were on the platform; but what did it mean? – there were the veritable Mr. Sammie Smiley and Mr. Johnnie Smith; but they looked fifteen or sixteen years older than when I saw them before, their hair being liberally sprinkled with gray.

To an old lady near me I remarked how strange it was that their hair should have thus turned gray in a few days. She looked at me wonderingly, and then smilingly replied, "You are probably a stranger: those two gentlemen have been gray for some years."

"But," I rejoined, "the last time I saw them, they were young, and had not a gray hair."

"Ah!" said the lady pleasantly; "but time will make us all gray. When those gentlemen commenced the agitation of man's rights, they were young; but twenty years has made a difference.

Twenty years! what did it mean? I had just begun to rub my eyes to see if I was asleep, as I have a habit of doing when dreaming any thing unpleasant, when Mr. Johnnie Smith came forward to speak. He demanded the franchise for men forthwith. He was clad in black velvet, but without trappings of any kind. While he was speaking, it seemed to me that I had the power of passing, unseen by the audience, from one speaker to the other, and looking into their thoughts. Some of them were so beautifully true and earnest, that I was delighted. Others were full of parade; and I saw written in their souls the word FASHIONABLE in large letters. In vain I asked myself, What does this mean? I could see no connection between this word and man's rights. But just then Mr. Johnnie Smith finished his speech by saying, "We are going to make man's rights FASHIONABLE!"

Then, in the twinkling of an eye, I seemed to see those gentlemen speakers stand up; and lo! how the majority were tricked off in finery! One, I remember, was dressed in pants of green-silk velvet, with little flounces of the same material from the foot to above the knees; a blue-velvet vest, with little flounces of green up to the pockets, and at a corresponding distance each side of the button-holes and buttons; a blue-velvet swallow-tailed coat, trimmed with green flounces and fringe down the front, round the sleeves, and round the coat-tails, which, under the influence of a "Grecian bend," were duly projected in the most fashionable style: the whole attitude, I am almost ashamed to say, suggesting that of a monkey standing on two feet, that had been accustomed to use four for that purpose. I must have laughed aloud in my sleep at this, so greatly did I feel amused. One glance around the platform showed that every gentleman on the platform attitudinized in a similar manner, except Mr. Sammie Smiley and Mr. Johnnie Smith.

But I must finish the description of this exquisitely fashionable young gentleman, whose name was Master Willie Sandy. Well, Master Willie's little head was graced with a little green-velvet cap in which were four blue feathers, pointing east, west, north, and south. In Master Willie's hands, which were covered by red gloves, was a tiny porte-monnaie, with the little chains of which his tapering fingers toyed while he spoke. On coming forward to address the audience, the projection of his coat-tails, in connection with his fashionable stoop, imparted the appearance of his being about to fly. But he talked very prettily on man's rights generally and particularly, even saying something in derogation of that fashionable life, which, as the poor boy had been taught, was the alpha and omega of existence. He concluded by stating that he was engaged in the study of engineering and of the higher branches of mathematics, and that he found nothing very difficult in either; at which remark some savans in the audience were vastly amused. He retired amidst loud applause, much of which was decidedly ironical. I was pained to hear such remarks as, "Willie better take off his Grecian bend;" "He had better take off his fashionable gear before he pretends to talk about the dignity of men, men's rights," &c.

Then another gentleman came to the front of the platform. He was tall for a man, dressed in gold and black, – black satin; suit trimmed with gold-colored-satin folds, with a Grecian bend of enormous size, so that his coat-tails projected yet more than those of Mr. Willie Sandy. He read a speech, or essay, on man's rights, which was very dry and uninteresting. Then followed a little gentleman dressed in black, without trimming of any kind. I saw he had a gold watch hung round his neck by a gold chain: a plain linen collar and cuffs completed his toilet. He remarked, that many colleges were now open to men, and that thousands and tens of thousands of young men educated therein had proved themselves equal to women; that governments should not be upheld merely to honor or create big-bugs, but more for the benefit of the governed, all of whom had a right to participate in making the laws. This was not a question as to whether men or women should be the governing class; but it was a question of *human* rights, *universal* rights, the rights of humanity.

"That is good," said several, as I moved again among the audience; "that was a sensible dress and a sensible speech." "What," asked another, "brings these fantastically dressed men on the platform?"

"Don't you know?" replied another; "why, Mr. Johnnie Smith and some others are resolved to make man's rights fashionable."

Then I thought in my dream that Mr. Sammie Smiley commenced to address the meeting; and I was so pleased that I can remember most of what he said. He began, –

"Friends, twenty years have passed away since we inaugurated this movement: many of us have grown gray in the cause. Allow me to give you an outline of its history. Almost simultaneously with its inauguration, a few of us came together, and, being desirous to begin at the beginning of man's wrongs, and save the generation of young children that were growing up around us, we commenced a 'Children's Rights Society.' We held meetings everywhere on this subject; gentlemen and ladies joined us, giving their time and money to the cause. Small were the beginnings; but thousands joined our ranks who were not, they said, believers in men's rights: man's rights brought its thousands, but children's rights its tens of thousands. Children's rights are the foundation of both man's and woman's rights; for we are laboring for the rights of humanity as a whole. In the first place, lectures were given to fathers and mothers on physiology. Halls were rented. We moved slowly, but surely. On every Saturday afternoon, lectures on scientific subjects were given to children. Science was simplified and illustrated by appropriate apparatus, and the children instructed in Nature's own method, not by *pouring in,* but by bringing out their own inherent powers. By degrees, halls were built in every large city, and devoted to the rights of children; and so successful were the methods of instruction adopted, that, in many places, they almost superseded our common schools.

"Allow me to specify a few examples. You all know the miserable methods of teaching that not long since were nearly universal: how science was fenced in by big words and obscure phraseology; you know how our children were confined six or seven hours daily in a dreary, miserable school-house, and how, as a general thing, the children hated the very idea of school. Now look into one of our large halls devoted to the rights of children. Observe the chemical room. A number of pneumatic troughs meet your eye, at each of which is a child making chemical experiments, with the aid and under the supervision of skillful professors.

"The geological room is furnished with large assortments of specimens. To every fifty children a tutor is assigned: they ramble through the country to collect specimens and observe the various formations, – excursion-trains being frequently engaged in taking them to distant localities to see for themselves hot springs, mountains, canyons, stalactites, stalagmites, &c. Ask those children if they like to study. In an instant they exclaim, 'Why, yes! it is delightful!'

"Physiology has been taught on the same principles: nothing has been held back. The uses of every organ of the body have been so explained, that, in relation thereto, the idea of vulgarity has disappeared, and secret vices have departed; for knowledge is power, – power to do right. Instead of the leaden eyes and feeble brain, our young men are vigorous, both in mind and body.

"Along with all this have been given lectures and lessons to adults; and, from morning to night, there are thousands in every city being educated in all that pertains to the laws of life.

"Twenty years have passed: those who were little children when we began have now grown to manhood and womanhood, and the majority of our young boys are now ready advantageously to exercise the franchise whenever they obtain it.

"Do you talk to me of the fashionable class, the moneyed class, who have all the time been either passive on-lookers or active opponents? Do you talk *now* of making man's rights *fashionable;* tricking out its advocates in the senseless gewgaws of fashionable society, and investing our reform with its weakness and folly?

"It can not be done. We have built our temple with divine corner-stones. While physiology has broken the physical bonds and bands with which fashion has bound us, enabling our boys and girls to be dressed in loose and comfortable clothing, our thoughts have been unbound and purified by corresponding mental training. Children of both sexes can be safely trusted to study together, play together, and when they grow to men and women, mingle together in all business relations, to the advantage of each and all.

"Though despised at first by some of the friends of man's rights, and regarded as a 'side issue,' having little or nothing to do with the main question, it having been held that we should confine ourselves to the advocacy of the franchise for men (which obtained, it was claimed that all the rest must follow), yet the movement for children's rights has been proved, by twenty years' experience, to have been the most powerful engine of success; for to-day there are millions of young men fully prepared judiciously to exercise the franchise, and millions of young women who have studied side by side with these young men, and are thus able, from personal knowledge, to realize the capacity of men, to acknowledge their rights, and to desire, that, in business, in politics, and in the household, they should continue to walk side by side.

"Children's rights — a branch, if you so please, of the man's rights movement — are, in fact, its foundation; while the right of franchise is the crown, the summit, the top-stone."

Round after round of applause followed the conclusion of his speech: so loud and so continued were the cheers, that I awoke, and lo! it was a dream.

Dream Number Five.

I HAVE just awakened from another visit to the land of dreams. So vivid is my recollection of every thing I saw and heard, that I am greatly inclined to the belief that I have visited one of the planets; and have been asking myself a number of questions, such as these: If time and space are almost nothing to the spirit, if spirit can travel more quickly than light, – yea, almost as quickly as thought, – may I not have visited one of the planets? And as the physical condition of the world so greatly resembled that of our own as to seem to me identical, and as the people were, in both physical and mental structure, so like ourselves, except that the women were superior to the men, I am more inclined to that idea than ever. On this, my last visit, I observed one or two very important facts: First, there was frost and snow; and second, the days and nights did not perceptibly differ in length from those of this earth. Hence, though I may subject myself to ridicule, though I may be laughed at as a visionary, I must own that I am inclined to believe that I have visited in my dream the planet Mars.

Another facts tends to substantiate this idea. I distinctly remember standing by my bedside as the dream terminated, and then awaking to the consciousness that my spirit stood there looking at my body asleep. It was but a moment certainly; but this double consciousness, in connection with the circumstances above mentioned, and others even more decisive, that will be hereafter specified, are such as to give a strong probability to the hypothesis, that, in this instance, the impossible (or what is currently deemed such) has been achieved, and even spectrum analysis (which embodies the latest developments in astronomical science) is outdone.

In this my last dream I found myself in a large public library; and who should enter but Mr. Sammie Smiley and Mr. Johnnie Smith, accompanied by two beautiful women. Then followed several ladies and gentlemen, whom I at once recognized as those I had seen at the meeting on man's rights. There, too, was the lady who had so amused and delighted the audience by her speech on man's inferiority. Then followed several introductions, from which I learned that said lady's name was Christiana Thistlewaite. She took from her pocket a newspaper, in which was a report (which she read) of a lecture delivered by an old woman who was on the editorial staff of a leading metropolitan paper. The lecturer considered that the recent extensive employment of men in stores in a neighboring city had proved detrimental to the morals of the sex; inasmuch as by opening up to them a prospect of support by their own labor, instead of being entirely dependent for a maintenance of their ability to secure a well-to-do wife, they became careless of their reputations, their independence thus tending to licentiousness. Mrs. Thistlewaite remarked, that, although she (Mrs. T.) was decidedly opposed to men transcending their legitimate sphere, she considered the lecturer's position highly absurd. "Poor old woman!" she added: "she has done good service in her day; always, until within a year or two, working for the poor and down-trodden, against the rich and powerful. She was especially useful in introducing co-operative households; but she is now evidently in her dotage. The paper can not afford to carry her many years longer, if it means to continue first-class.

"While they talked together, and looked at the books, some of them reclining in easy-chairs or on lounges, with books in their hands, I opened a very large, handsome book, which I found to be a Bible. "Well," I said, "this is just what I want;" so I opened it, and began to look over the passages of Scripture which referred to woman. I was astonished – nay, shocked – to find, at the very commencement, that the whole history of the fall of man was reversed as to the sexes. *Adam* was tempted by the serpent, and gave the forbidden fruit to his wife; for which reason it was said to the man that "she [the woman] shall rule over thee," and "in sorrow thou [the man] shall attend to the children;" that a virtuous man was a crown to his wife, and his price above rubies; "he layeth his hands to the spindle, and his hands hold the distaff;" his *wife* being known in the gates, when *she* sat among the elders of the land, &c. Farther on it was stated that husbands should obey their wives, as the head of the man was the woman, even as Christ was the head of the church; that it was not becoming that a man should speak in the church; but, if they would know any thing, let them ask their wives at home. "Why," I said to myself, "this Bible has certainly been translated and probably compiled by women; for no *man* in this land would have so interpreted the Scriptures against his sex. Thus the women have strengthened themselves behind the Bible; and so the poor down-trodden men are held in slavery by means of this book, thus interpreted!"

While turning over the leaves, Mrs. Christiana Thistlewaite came to my side, to whom I said, "Are all your Bibles like this, madam?" at the same time pointing to some of the preceding passages. She smiled as she replied, "Certainly; they are all alike. Our Bible is translated from the languages in which it was originally written: wise, good women were the translators; and I would like Mr.

Sammie Smiley and Mr. Johnnie Smith to see those passages of Scripture."

"Those passages," rejoined the former gentlemen, "were never intended to be used to keep men in an inferior position, or to deprive them of their just rights. Those who wrote the books in the Bible, like you, did not believe in man's rights; and they wrote as they believed. God never said those men were inferior to women; for in Christ there was neither bond nor free, male nor female (Gal. iii. 28); but all were one. God, in his works, never utters the word *inferior;* the sun shines and the flowers grow for all; the earth brings forth enough of its fruits for all, the varied diversities of manifestation beautifully blending into one unity of design: and as the varied contrasts and diversities and blending of color in a painting produce a unity of expression, no *color* being inferior or superior to any other, so Nature and art alike belie any written word implying *inferiority* of one sex to another, whatever may be the *diversities.* Who says that God has made one sex inferior to another utters a blasphemy."

Here several ladies gathered around Mr. Sammie Smiley and Mrs. Christiana Thistlewaite.

"We," continued the gentleman, "have only to ask our own common sense what is right or wrong with respect to man or woman, even as was asked by an ancient reformer, once abhorred, now adored (nominally), 'Why even of yourselves judge ye not what is right?' (Luke xii. 57). You, ladies, have made the laws, and you have made them to suit yourselves; think you, that, if men as well as women had the making of the laws, in marriage the man would have no control over property previously belonging to him, unless secured to him by a special deed? Realize, ladies, if you can, what would be your condition were the legal status of the sexes reversed! If a man owns property or has a store, he is wronged by having no voice in the laws or regulations of the town or city in which he resides. If the wife die, the husband has the use only during life of *one-third* of their joint property. If the *husband* dies, however, the wife takes *absolute possession* of the *whole*. Man is thus wronged by being denied the right of franchise; even the *children* of the widower being in many cases subjected to the control of strange women appointed by a court, instead of that of the remaining parent."

Mrs. Susan Thistlewaite then said to Mr. Johnnie Smith, "Allow me, sir, to ask a question. Why do gentlemen, when they meet each other, occupy the time entirely in frivolous conversation about love, marriage, &c.?"

"Admitting," replied Mr. Smith, "the generality and absurdity of the practice, it must be considered as an unavoidable result of the conditions inaugurated and upheld by those who would circumscribe man's sphere, and limit his faculties to affairs, that, when exclusively followed, tend to dwarf the faculties, and make people narrow and gossiping. You, ladies, would do the same were you in our position. Close to you, ladies, as you have closed to us, all avenues to honor and emolument; deprive you of education and pecuniary independence, making you dependent on the bounty of man; and would not the most important subject to you be marriage?"

"Mr. Johnnie Smith is right," I replied, as I stepped into the very midst of them. "In the land where I reside, *men* have all the rights which you ladies have in this country: men make the laws and oppress women, just as, in this land of yours, women make the laws and oppress men."

"Oh, oh! astonishing!" exclaimed several. "Do tell us something about things there."

"Well," I continued, "ladies are the housekeepers."

"Ridiculous!" interjected two or three ladies.

"Ladies do all the sewing and knitting."

How they laughed!

"The men hold the colleges, and are educated therein, only a few being open to women: the majority of ladies are educated at common schools, and a few at boarding-schools."

"Ha, ha! oh, ho! boarding-schools for ladies! fine education that must be for women!"

"Go on, go on!" called out several; "I never heard any thing so ridiculous! Ha, ha, ha!"

"Men hold the purse, pay car-fares, pay for refreshments, and stand when the cars are crowded, while the ladies sit. Men dress in plain clothes, while women are walking advertisements of dry goods; men wear their hair generally short and clean, while women not only wear their own hair, but add to it quantities of horse-hair, grease, and other materials, making of the whole a putrid, uncomfortable, disgusting mass. Our women decorate themselves, too, with ribbons, as do your men, and have their fashion-books; their dresses far excelling in absurd ugliness and unhealthfulness any thing worn by your men."

"Is it possible? how outrageously absurd and repulsive!" they exclaimed; while a ringing laugh filled the library, and more ladies entered. "Go on, go on!" said several.

"Men, and only men, make the laws, as senators, representatives, judges, &c. No women vote or legislate: in short, the whole matter is reversed."

"How are the women intellectually?" asked a lady.

"As a general rule," I replied, "they are just in the condition that men are here. By a singular coincidence, an old man who edits a leading metropolitan journal in my country recently delivered a lecture (at a place called Bethlehem, I think), in which he took the same position, as regards the employment of women in stores, and their morals, that your old-woman editor is reported to have taken in regard to the employment of men in stores here. The objection is probably equally well founded in both cases; and the parallelism is so far complete, that our editor is getting to be termed an old woman or old granny; those terms with us being used to designate weakness in intellectual or executive operations."

Then Mr. Sammie Smiley stepped on a chair, and began: "Friends, you have heard what the stranger has told us. What do you think of it? Does it not prove my position that those ladies would be no wiser or better than we are, were they in our position? And does it not prove conclusively that not sex, but *condition,* is the root of the matter?"

"I do not believe the story told us by the stranger," said Mrs. Thistlewaite. "Man superior to woman! men legislate! Oh! it won't bear the light of day for an instant!"

"Where is that stranger?" said several voices. I had entered a large room opening from the library, and was looking at several portraits of distinguished stateswomen; for no man's face was among them. When I heard the inquiry, I returned to the library. Then the crowd gathered around me in great curiosity. "So you live in a land," said one lady, "where men have their rights, do you?"

"Yes," I said.

"And do you mean to say that you were never permitted to vote?"

"I never was permitted; but I have protested against the exclusion."

"What is the name of your land?" asked several.

"The United States of North America."

"Where is that?"

"Do you ask where it is?" I replied; "why, look at your maps."

"Here is a map of the world," said Christiana Thistlewaite.

I went up to the map and looked it over; and, lo! it was not like our maps at all. There were the frigid zones, the equator and the ecliptic, the parallels of longitude and latitude, the tropics and the poles, to which were even added many isothermal lines; but the distribution of the land and water was very different in many parts, though in others maintaining something of a general resemblance.

"This map is not correct," I said.

Then arose a general derisive laugh. "I am very sorry," said Mrs. Christiana Thistlewaite. "It would have given me great satisfaction to see that land of man's rights, my friend; but it has vanished! it is not to be found on the map! Ah!" she continued in bitter sarcasm, "it is too bad that the beautiful land where men are the lords of creation, where men are the superior race, and women the inferior, can not be found."

Confused and astonished by the map, confused and astonished by these puzzling remarks, I awoke. The map, however, had made such an impression on my mind, that I drew an outline of it at once; then I consulted a friend of mine versed in astronomy, to whom I showed the diagram. He took down a strange work containing some excellent engravings of the planets as viewed through telescopes of the highest magnifying powers, and one of them corresponded, in the distribution of land and water, exactly to my diagram. Yes, there was my Dreamland, there my planet, – the planet *Mars*!

Dream Number Six.

The following four additional "dreams" were added when *Man's Rights; or, How Would You Like It?* was reprinted in *Woodhull and Claflin's Weekly*, New York, Sep 3-Nov 19, 1870.

I HAVE just awoke. What a bad night! How it rains! Why, it is pouring down.

Once again I have been to my dreamland, where the respective conditions of men and women are reversed. My watch lies on the table and its pointers tell me it is five minutes past two o'clock. My husband is sound asleep. Sleep on, my dear, good fellow! Don't open your eyes until my dream is written down. But I must write down the two headings at once, before they are forgotten:

The Delirium Protest and the Sheepman-Yellow-Green Protest.

There! I am glad they are down before my memory has any chance to prove treacherous. Dear me! my husband awakes.

"Why, Annie, what are you doing at midnight, with that gas burning? You know I cannot sleep with a light in the room. Writing! What in the world are you doing writing at midnight?"

"I have had another dream," I replied; "so please don't say another word. Just turn on the other side, then the gas will not shine in your face." There – he has done so; good, obliging fellow! So now to my dream, in which it seemed to me I had the power of hovering in the atmosphere. Below me was the city which I had so often visited, and there, as heretofore, were the gentlemen parading the streets, their elaborately trimmed coats, pants and vests emulating the colors of the rainbow. With astonishment I beheld that beneath every coat-tail was a Grecian bend, which caused said caudalities to project at an angle of forty-five degrees. Many of these "well dressed" gentlemen were accompanied by dignified ladies, whose beauty, dress and carriage all denoted that women were there decidedly the superior sex. "Oh, sad sight!" I said to myself. "Oh, terrible condition for man!" Then, as my heart went out to them in pity and commiseration, I found myself walking in the broad, beautiful avenue of that city; and it seemed to me, as it had often seemed before, that I had the power to look into the minds of these poor men, and also into the minds of those grand, beautiful women. I found that many of those degraded men were planning cajolery and deceit, by means of which they expected to extract money from their wives for the purchase of costly suits of clothing. As they occasionally lingered to observe the beautifully-embroidered vests, the elegantly-trimmed coats and other extravagant paraphernalia peculiar to man's wardrobe there, I saw that, in many instances, their mental structure was essentially inferior to that of women, and that this was a necessary result of inherited degradation. I then thought of Darwin's observations and experiments, proving that in certain species of ants and other animals, peculiarities of sexes are transmitted, so that what one sex inherits the other does not; and I said to myself, "Here is a terrible exemplification of this principle in the *genus homo*, for this inferiority has even permeated cerebral tissues."

But at that moment I remembered the Man's Rights meeting which I had attended, the noble men I had seen there, and the great speech of Mr. Sammy Smiley, which proved that many men were, and many men might be, equal to the best of women, and I inwardly exclaimed, "Thank God for man's rights!" Then my attention was called to large posters on the walls, around which troops of little, fantastically-dressed gentlemen had gathered.

"Sheepman-Yellow-Green Protest" met my eye in one place, while on the opposite corner, in yet larger head letters, I saw "Delirium Protest".

The little darling gentlemen tittered and laughed as they read. "That is good, that is excellent for those men's rights folks!" exclaimed one of them. "I will certainly sign that."

Just them a young girl came along with an armful of papers which she began to distribute to these gentlemen and also to the passers by. One found its way into my hands, and lo, it was the Sheepman-Yellow-Green Protest. I put on my spectacles and read about as follows.

"The petition of the undersigned gentlemen to the Congress of the United Republics protesting against the extension of the suffrage to men.

"We, the undersigned gentlemen, do most respectfully appeal to your honorable body against the extension of the suffrage to men. We shrink from notoriety, and would fain hide ourselves from woman's eye, well knowing that it is man's place to be modest and shame faced, but we are deeply and powerfully impressed by the grave facts which threaten our happiness in view of the proposed granting of the franchise to men.

"Because the Bible says that woman was made first, then man, proving conclusively that woman was superior to man.

[This reminded me of the idea enunciated by Burns, that Nature "tried her prentice hand on man, and then she made the lasses, O!" but I read on.]

"Because as men we find enough care and responsibility in taking care of our homes, our children, our sewing and knitting, and other *et ceteras* of man's life, and we don't feel strong enough, mentally or physically, to assume other and heavier burdens such as an extension of suffrage to man would bring.

"Because the possession of the franchise would be detrimental to the workingmen of our country, especially sewing men, creating among them a discontent and dissatisfaction which would never be assuaged until they should find their way to offices of honor and emolument, which, we all know, belong exclusively to women.

"Because the extension of the franchise to man would be terribly detrimental to the marriage relation, resulting in two heads to a family instead of one, and causing married persons who, by reason of mutual unfitness, should never have formed that relation to each other, to seek for its dissolution though bound to each other by the holy ties of matrimony.

"Because no general law affecting the condition of all men should be enacted to meet the exceptional discontent of workingmen who are needed to perform the labor and drudgery of the world, nor of bachelors, who ought, like ourselves, to have married honorable and respectable women well able to provide for them comfortable homes and all the luxuries of life.

"For these and many other equally important reasons do we beg of your wisdom that no law extending the franchise to the men of our country may be passed.

"[Signed] Mr. Jemima D. Hykoolorum, Mr. Josephine Rooster-Schmidt, Mr. Rev. Doctor Martha Manton, Mr. Rev. Dr. Jerusa Bottler, Mr. Rev. Dr. Patience Rankskin, Mr. Betsy B. English, Master Johnnie Carrott, Mr. Catherine V. Morecold, Mr. Sarah McCowlick, Mr. Senator Mary Shearman, Mr. Senator Jayne Tocsin, Mr. Senator Caroline Telrock, Mr. Lucretia T. Troppick, Mr. Cynthia Walksome, Master Charlie E. Birching."

As I finished the names I looked up, and there was Christiana Thistlethwaite before me. "Good morning, my friend," she said; "I am glad to see you perusing that document. As you have probably perceived, the Sheepman-Yellow-Green Protest is signed by the husbands of the most honorable and respectable women in our country – husbands of Senators and clergymen. Come, walk with me to the Senate," she added; and in an instant I found myself in the reception room of that body.

With the "Delirium Protest" in my hand, I took a chair, readjusted my spectacles and began to look it over. I found it was signed by one hundred and forty-one men (oh, these poor deluded men) of a *Dorain* or *Norain* county – I have forgotten the exact name. The following paragraphs caught my eye:

"We men acknowledge no inferiority to women."

Pretty good! I said to myself; "pretty good! You one hundred and forty-one men are in a very hopeful condition. But I will give, as nearly as I can render it, the *Delirium Protest*.

"We believe that God has wisely made men to be husbands, to stay at home, to take care of the children, to look after and keep in repair the wardrobes of the family and attend to all the little etceteras the sum of which makes home comfortable and attractive, these duties being even implied in the very construction and derivation of the word, *Houseband*.

"We believe that God has made woman to legislate, to govern and to fill every department of lucrative labor, and that each sex is well adapted to the duties of each.

"We believe that God has ordained that every man who has not a wife to provide for him is an outcast, and unworthy of our consideration. [Well done, Podsnap.]

"We feel that our domestic cares, our homes, our children, making and receiving calls, studying the fashions and so arranging our household and clothing that the apparent effect is that of having twice or thrice the income really received, fill up the whole measure of our time, abilities and needs.

"We believe that our duties, as above-defined, are as sacred as any upon earth.

"We feel that those duties are such as no woman could perform, constituting *prima facto* evidence that God has wisely adapted each sex to its special duties.

"The importance of our duties, as above-defined, urge us to protest against being compelled to accept the franchise, or any of its resultant duties, which could not be performed without sacrificing some duties exclusively appertaining to our sex, and which we therefore feel under obligations to perform.

"Our mothers, sisters, wives and daughters represent us at the ballot box; our mothers and sisters love us; our wives are our choice [happy souls!] and are with us; our daughters are what we made them, and we are content. (oh, bliss supreme!) We are content that they represent us at the ballot box, in scientific pursuits, in the lecture room and in the world of business and legislation – in short, in everything that would divert us from our home and domestic duties, as above defined. We are content to represent them in our primary schools, at our firesides, telling stories and amusing the children, warming our wives' slippers and preparing the dressing-robes for their return home; and we well know that in this way, by the influence we thus gain over our wives, we are better represented, even at the ballot box, than we possibly could be were all men allowed to vote."

"Happy one hundred and forty-one!" I said to myself, as I took off my spectacles; "peace be to your ashes."

Then I looked about the large reception room of the Senate; there were young men and old men, in all their finery and frivolity – ribbons and ruffles, trills and flounces – whispering and tittering, swinging and prancing on their little toes, every motion giving perspicuity to Grecian bends and long coat tails; their hands were squeezed into small gloves, which gave them a cats' paw appearance. As they walked to and fro, or stood in groups, their little gossamer fans fluttered like the wings of as many butterflies.

The pages of the Senate were young girls, whose countenances bloomed with health and intelligence; and I observed that they were busily engaged carrying to Senators in the Senate chamber dainty, perfumed cards of these delicate little gentlemen. Never had I witnessed so sad a sight. Never for an instant did I cease sorrowing for those poor downtrodden men, whom I well knew were capable of filling every department here monopolized by women.

As I sat there watching the visitors at the reception room, a Senator, in her stately robes of plain black, without any ornaments, entered from the Senate chamber; then three or four of those frivalous creatures I have described minced and bowed, fluttered and chattered, while she, like a superior being, graciously listened, occasionally making a remark. Two rows of parchment, tied with blue ribbon, were handed her by one of those little gents. As she unfolded first one and then the other, her eyes rapidly scanning their contents, I saw in large letters on one, "Sheepman-Yellow-Green Protest," and on the other "Delirium Protest."

"But I believe in Man's Rights," I heard the Senator say.

"O, blessed moment!" I said to myself, as a tear rolled down my face; "there is one noble, beautiful soul, brave enough to say she believes in the rights of these poor, degraded men, who in my world are considered the lords of creation."

Then I reflected, as I sat there on my chair, on the similarity in names, in sentiments and logic between those protests and some that whilom appeared in the papers here signed by the wives of divers high mightinesses in Washington, Elyria and elsewhere, denouncing *woman's* rights, and I concluded that this remarkable parrallelion must be; and the manifestation of that general law of correspondences under which certain changes in the sun are said by savans to be concurrent with magnetic and meteoric terrestrial disturbances; and might also have a bearing on the theory of a Parisian bachelor who devoted his life to the investigation of humps, and who, from numerous facts which he had ascertained in all quarters of the globe, concluded that the forms of such protuberances corresponded with the more or less hilly character of the countries in which they respectively originated.

While intensely occupied in these philosophical comparisons, and endeavoring to apply them to reformatory operations in both worlds I became so bewildered that I awoke.

Why, it has taken me over an hour to write this dream; the rain is still pouring. I am sleepy, and must retire.

Dream Number Seven.

MY noble husband has just delivered himself of the following speech:

"There you are! Up again at midnight! Another dream, I suppose! Well, this is becoming quite a serious matter! You will forget your dreams if you don't write them down at once! Indeed! These are Woman's Rights times with a vengeance, and no mistake, when I cannot rest in my bed at night without being disturbed by my wife in this manner!

"Now I will give you a little of my mind: You are a dreamer, and nothing but a dreamer, and henceforth you may rise fifty times in the night, or you may sit up all night to write your dreams if you choose; *but you shall not do it at my cost.* I believe in Individual Sovereignty. You shall go to some other room."

"All right, all right, my dear, amiable husband," I replied, with a good-natured laugh, at the same time taking up my paper, pen and ink, putting out the gas and quietly making my way to the sitting-room. So here I am, all alone. Henceforth if I should have any more need to write in the night here I will come at once; my dear, good, abused husband rest in peace!

But I must relate my dream in which I again found myself in the before-mentioned city, and in a gentleman's dressing-room. Before a large mirror, which appeared to be let into the walls, and which reached from the top of the room to the floor, stood a little gentleman in his long night-dress, his hair full of curl-papers, for the quantity of paper greatly exceeded that of the hair. As I was noting the beautiful needlework that profusely trimmed his night-dress, and which, I perceived, had been done by his own delicate fingers, like the strange incongruity of dreams, there began to move into the room, one after another, a great number of gentlemen in their long night-dresses and abundant curl-papers. As I stood on one side, I found that they were entering a large assembly dressing-room, as large as the reception-room of the White House. I observed, too, that on every side and down the centre of this room were arranged, side by side, all necessary articles for a gentlemen's dressing-room, as if the contents of a few score of small ones such as I had just seen had been consolidated and rearranged with reference to the maximum of convenience and minimum of labor. What elegant nightdresses, I said to myself as they passed! And yet, though I admired them in the abstract, I felt something, I am sorry to say, akin to contempt for these gentlemen whose forms they covered.

One fat gentleman so loaded down with avoirdupoise as to suggest by his breathing a little steam engine, the wonder of my childhood days, named, "Puffing Billy," came waddling along in a night-gown having four ruffles round the lower portion and tucks innumerable. He had very little hair. I then confidently believe that in half an hour every hair on his little head could have been counted!

Each gentleman as he passed me, and seemed to be in his accustomed place, carried in his hand a pair of corsets and a long, black *something* that looked to me very like a horsetail. The corsets I could comprehend; but what were they going to do with these horses' tails? Then another puzzling feature of this strange scene was that where they did not carry these appendages they carried an armful of tow, or sheep's wool, or what looked to me very like these substances.

By-and-by all seemed to have entered; for the doors were closed and those night-gowned gentlemen, attended by young men whom they called their servant boys, or dressing boys, prepared to dress.

There was something in the countenances of these gentlemen that impressed me very disagreeably. Almost invariably their skin was spotted with yellow, and, as a whole, looked dark, dried and unnaturally shrivelled. Two exceptions to this rule were so grateful to my love of the beautiful that I lingered round about these two gentlemen some time. These two I had observed on entering the room, as they carried no corsets in their hands; and the diameter of their waists suggested the idea that they would form models for the men of that world as excellent as the Venus de Medici does for the women of this world.

But what a scene that dressing-room! what a medley! what confusion of odors as the dressing progressed – of perfumes, grease, pomatum, powders, rouge, hair dye, and I know not what other substances for cleanliness and hygiene!

A servant boy whom I had seen standing at the head of the room with a something in his hand – I had not observed what – here sounded a gong, and in an instant the hair dressing commenced. Then I perceived for what were designed the supposed horses' tails, also the tow, sheep's wool and several other strange, dark masses which had seemed wholly inappropriate, for anything connected with the toilet; for lo, all these were mounted on the tops and backs of their little heads, making them look as if they had exchanged their own heads for those of horses, minus the dignity usually appertaining to those animals. Oh, sad sight! said I to myself; oh, terrible result of man's degradation!

This gear on the head and its adjustment consumed considerable time, and as it progressed I felt a strange, stilled sensation, caused, I presume, by the numerous odors of that assembly dressing-room.

Then twelve men entered the room carrying before them on waiters a number of small white cups, some containing white, others red or pink powder; also, several small, broad silvered knives and sundry tiny brushes. "Ah, here comes the porcelainists! Here are the porcelainists!" I heard several voices exclaim with a pleased flutter, as with small brushes they were painting their eyebrows.

Simultaneously as they entered twelve gentlemen took seats together in the centre of the room – twelve blotched, wrinkled, yellow faces! I looked at them, then at the twelve porcelainists, and then at the cups, into which was being poured some liquid from a bottle. What can be the meaning of all this? I asked myself in astonishment; but the mystery was soon explained: for like magic the small knives in the hands of the porcelainists transferred the contents of the cups to the faces of the twelve gentlemen sitting in a row. Over the forehead and cheeks, over and round about the nose and close to the corner of the mouth went the knives, covering up ugliness instanter. In ten minutes the twelve faces reminded me of the little porcelain dolls sold in our stores.

"You must not laugh, or romp, dear gentlemen," said one of the operators; "you will mar your faces; guard against all emotions, as well, as against any other agency causing sudden and extreme movements of the features; for by allowing such movements or emotions you would cause the porcelain to crack and spoil it completely. Don't move, please, for a few minutes; it takes a little time for the porcelain, after being laid on the face, to dry thoroughly." Very obediently the twelve faces kept exactly in one position. During the operation quite a circle of half-dressed gentlemen had gathered round.

"Beautiful! beautiful!" I heard them exclaim; "Sweet! pretty!" said one; "Delightful!" said another; but I thought contemptuously: "I would like to suspend you twelve between heaven and earth as a spectacle to gods, to angels and to men!"

One of these beautiful (!) twelve, who evidently was suffering from a bad cold, here began to sneeze. Dear, dear! how he did sneeze! and as he sneezed the porcelain began to crack in several places, and small pieces fell to the floor. Oh, hideous sight!

But hark! the gong sounds again. (How I do hate a gong), and then a hundred corsets, embracing as many gentlemen's bodies (including the elect twelve, who were prudently conserving their new faces) were subjected to superlative pressure. Tight, tighter and yet tighter were they compressed until not only the faces of the attendant servant boys, but those of the gentlemen being laced were red with the effort. As the lacing progressed the respiration became more difficult.

But what next? the gong sounds again! "Dressing the feet!" Why, the man calls out this as he might the figures of a dance! [What absurdity there is in dream!]

Then I thought I was greatly puzzled while I wondered I had not previously observed that some of these gentlemen wore on their feet what (for want of a better name) I shall call a *foot-vice*. This was a curious apparatus, with straps and buckles, worn on the feet during the night for the purpose of moulding the foot into a rounded form. This result had, in a few instances, been so completely obtained that the sides of the foot were rounded over and almost met on the under part of the foot. Of course those who had servant boys required them when dressing their feet; and when the *foot-vice* had been used two servant boys were brought into requisition, one of whom kept the foot in its rolled condition while the other commenced to introduce the foot into the gaiter. This was a difficult feat, for it required a long time and several trials before completion.

But I am weary: perhaps sleepy; so I shall not attempt to describe the numerous divisions of the toilet indicated by that terrible gong; the putting on of "Grecian bends" was one. May I never see such a sight again! No wonder that when dressed their coat tails projected at an angle of forty-five degrees!

Never shall I forget when the gong sounded for the false teeth to be introduced into the mouth; for it seemed in my dream that there came to me at the same moment the power to see and examine the internal organs of every gentleman present. In all who wore corsets (and there were only two gentlemen who did not), I saw that the five lower ribs were contracted, and in some cases overlapped; that the air-cells in the lower part of the lungs were rendered inactive by compression, and that in consequence of the sympathy existing between all organs of the body, there was very observable either positive indications of disease or great weakness. One young gentleman, who had been originally healthy, I perceived was paralyzed in his right arm, and very shortly would be paralyzed on one side of the body from the use of the foot-vice; and that the waist, though originally of proper circumference, was gradually approaching that of the wasp.

Then, as previously in a former dream, I looked into the spirit, saw the links connecting the body with the spirit, and as by a glance was enabled to go back in time by means of these links through several generations of ancestors. Carefully and accurately *past* ancestral endowment – physical, moral and mental – were compared with those before me, especially were the co-relations of parts observed, and I perceived that it had come to be a fact, indeed, that *those* gentlemen, at least, were inferior to woman.

Oh, saddening realization! Oh, poor, silly butterfly men! Verily in this land man is inferior to woman!

Thus was I sadly meditating when the scene changed and I found myself in the home of Mrs. Christiana Thistlewaite, with Mr. Johnny Smith and Mr. Sammy Smiley as her guests.

"Dear friend," she said, taking my hand, "I am very glad to see you; do you know that I am a convert to Man's Rights?"

"You!" I exclaimed, with great astonishment.

"Yes, I am convinced that the demands of the Man's Rights Society are founded in nature."

"But how has this come to pass?" I inquired.

"I will tell you, dear friend," she replied, as she took a chair near me, still retaining my hand in her own. "You remember the *Sheepman Yellow-Green Protest;* also the *Delirium Protest?*"

"Certainly."

"Very well; I read them over carefully, and was dissatisfied. I saw that they would not bear the light of day for an instant, then I tried to find better reasons for denying to men their claimed rights. I gave my best thoughts and attention to the subject, and to make a long story short, as the result of that thought, here I am a thorough believer in *Man's Rights.* So you see the *Sheepman Yellow-Green Protest* and *Delirium Protest* have done more good, in one case, at least, than the silly men who penned it ever conceived."

I commenced to express my delight at the change in her sentiments, when she remarked: "But you are very sad, my friend; you show it in every lineament of your face." Then I thought in my dream that I related all I had witnessed in the assembly dressing room, dwelling very minutely on the peculiar and diversified ancestral endowments handed down from generation to generation, and the culture of expression these had received in each, and finally the conclusions forced upon me of the real inferiority of man to woman.

"Don't be cast down, dear friend," replied Christiana Thistlewaite; "you have only chanced to meet some of the worst specimens of our men. This class of men does not represent more than one-fiftieth of the male sex. You must know that this is a large country, composed of many races, some inferior, but many superior. These you have visited are only one race, and a very small race – the *fashionable* race; and I am glad, truly glad, of their *foot-vices,* their waist-vices, their cosmetics, paints, powders and porcelain, for they all form such powerful *brain*-vices and life-annihiliators that in less than a century every one of their descendants will be swept from the face of our planet. Inferior races must give place to superior; and I thank our Father for this beautiful law." As she finished, she led me into a large, handsome room in which were gathered probably two hundred persons of both sexes. "Now use your *'soul-gift,'* dear friend," she said, "and tell me of *this* race of men and women." I did so. I comprehended the capacities of each brain, of each spirit, and then walked down the aisles of time for many generations of ancestors; divined the physical, mental and spiritual heritage that had passed from generation to generation with the added culture or repression of such heritage, and contrasted these results in the male sex with the results obtained by the same means in the female sex; and as I followed from cause to effect, from added growth to added growth, there came to my own spirit a blessed peace. Here was no inferiority, no retrogression; but in characters ineffaceable were written, for both man and woman, possibilities and capabilities as far transcending the present as those of the present transcended those of the long ago, even a million of ages.

Dream Number Eight.

NOT to the planet Mars did my dream take me this time, but on board a sailing vessel just entering New York bay. Very foggy it had been for days; but the clouds having just lifted, to my delightful eyes were revealed the shores of Staten Island and the other components of the brilliant *tout ensemble* greeting the voyager as he approached the metropolitan cities which bounded the distance.

My husband and I had for years been in some remote corner of the earth, where we had never received any news either of home, friends or country; but where that out-of-the-way place could have been situated, impenetrable not only to telegraph and post, but beyond the reach even of "our own correspondent," I could not remember. In vain I tried to recall its name and locality, or even the least incident which had befallen us in our long exile – the years we had spent there were all a blank. However, I did know that our home was in New York city, and that very soon we should be there. In vain did I interrogate my husband as to where we had been; he only looked wonderingly in my face, laughed heartily several times, and said: "I really cannot remember. All I know is that we have been gone from the United States ten years, and that shortly we shall be again in New York city. Yonder is a tug boat," he continued, pointing to one evidently making for us; "I am very anxious to hear the news. Oh, to get the sight of a New York paper once more!"

How vividly do I remember this part of my dream! – how recall every moment of time, and every feature of the beautiful scene before us. Land, land once more, bringing thoughts of home, joyous expectations of meeting dear friends from whom we had been long separated, and all the palpitating expectancy that seemed to make my whole being throb with delight.

By and by the tug-boat reached us, and my husband realized his millennium by feasting his eyes on a New York paper, in his haste to obtain which he came very near falling overboard. A newspaper man to his very bones, his existing for so many years without access to that seeming necessary of life had been to me a mystery almost as great as would have been a fish living a like period without water.

"Der teufel! sacre tonnerre! was ist? place aux dames?" exclaimed he facetiously, as his eye scanned the contents; "what changes ten years have brought about! A lady president three months in office, and yet the world goes around as usual! I rather expect to see, when we get to the city, that the people are walking on their heads; the world must be turned upside down!"

"You mean that ten years has turned the world 'right side up,' with care?"

"Just as you like," he replied, with a good-natured smile; "but I was never more astonished in my life."

"There must be Congresswomen, then," I said, as a feeling of wholesome pride was born into my soul; women were something after all. How distinctly I remember the feeling of importance that leaped into existence within me, and that remains with me at this moment, though I now know that it was only a dream.

Then my husband handed me the paper. "Read for yourself," he said; "nearly one half of the United States Senate, and fully one half of the House, are women." Then he laughed, rubbed his hands, stood on his feet, lifted his hat and said to me, as he bowed profoundly, "I salute you, dear madame, in deference to the glorious achievement of woman. May she never descend from the height to which she has attained!"

"I thank you," I replied, "in the name of every woman. Oh, I no more want to be a man, but rejoice that I am a woman."

"Hurrah for our side of the house," replied my merry husband. Then he looked around, saying, "How I wish that tug boat would hurry up; no more ten years spent in — confound it! what *IS* the name of that place? Strange that I can't recollect, when I was always so ready with names and locations. Is my brain softening, or what *can* be the trouble? Well, no matter what it is, we will live henceforth in the United States, and die there too, when it comes to that. 'Better fifty years of Europe than a cycle of Cathay.' We reach here just in time to enjoy the woman government and observe its constituent parts."

All in my dream was very consistent until we landed on the wharf, and then, like the crazyness of dreams, no surprise was expressed or felt on finding it suddenly midnight and myself and husband just afterward walking up Broadway as leisurely as if it had been a pleasant afternoon in October.

By and by we looked up and saw a number of men approaching; they filled the sidewalk, so we stepped aside under a lamp and saw them pass. All were evidently in charge of policemen; several were handcuffed and acting like madmen. More, and yet more, passed us, so that we could hardly walk a block without being compelled to step aside, which we always did near a lamp post.

"What does this mean?" I asked my husband.

"It means, I suppose, woman's government."

"Oh, stop your nonsense," I replied, laughing; adding, "I believe the inmates of some lunatic asylum are being removed, perhaps to another asylum."

All this time we were scanning the faces of the gentlemen (for they were all gentlemen) as they passed under the gaslight. Then my husband recognized several whom he had formerly known, one of whom, Mr. — was a senator when we left, ten years previously. I almost gave his name, but that wouldn't do. There were two reverend gentlemen, but I must be still more circumspect in regard to names, because in case of an action for slander, their congregations could fee so many lawyers that I should certainly get the worst of it; besides which, I should lose the good opinion of the religious press, which to me is very dear! Besides, I might even be suspected of heterodoxy, which would be terrible!!

But, *rerenons à nos moutons*, even if they are black sheep, with possibly a sprinkling of goats. It was a strange scene, for all classes of men appeared to be represented. Not only the lowest, or those on whose countenances the mark of the beast was distinctly imprinted, but also the respectable, the religious, and even the intellectual and cultivated. Men were there with fine countenances, and with heads that phrenologists would have declared those of statesmen and philosophers. Why were such men accompanied by policemen? Why these wholesale arrests?

All at once I exclaimed, "Oh, dear! there! see! dear, good, elder Stiggins! Oh, dear! see! a policeman has him handcuffed; save, save him, husband!" I did not, however, wait for my husband to do anything, but rushed into the crowd. "There is some mistake," I exclaimed; "O, dear, dear Elder Stiggins!" taking his hand in my own; but the crowd pushed on, and with difficulty did I make my escape.

Then my dream, without any connecting link, landed me in a comfortable room in a large hotel. On a table near my husband was a large collection of newspapers, evidently a file extending back some years. He was greedily devouring them, scanning one after another, and then throwing them on the floor to make way for their successors. By-and-by he began to laugh – how he did laugh!

"What is the matter?" I asked; "tell me, what is it?"

"Excellent! good! first rate! happy thought!"

"Well, tell me! what is it?" Then he tried to smooth his face and answer:

"Why, it appears that one of the first acts of both Houses of Congress, after the inauguration of President — was to pass a law providing that henceforth, in the District of Columbia, no woman prostitute should be arrested, fined, imprisoned, sent to Magdalen asylums for reformation or otherwise molested, but that all laws punishing prostitution in women should, from and after the passage of the Act, be enforced against their male companions. A similar law was soon afterward passed in the State of New York. The Washington authorities, however, regarded it only as a huge joke intended by Congressmen for electioneering effect among their lady constituents. I have not yet reached any information as to its enforcement in this State."

Then he again vigorously betook himself to a fresh instalment of newspapers, and having ground up a dozen or so in his mental mill, fastened on another. "They intend the law to go into effect here," he remarked. "Three large houses for the reformation of prostitute men are being built." As he said this he handed me the newspaper, and pointed out the heading:

THREE LARGE HOUSES BEING BUILT FOR THE
REFORMATION OF PROSTITUTE MEN!!
MALE MAGDALENS!!!

"We laugh, my dear," I said, "because it is novel, but there is justice and wisdom in the law."

"Yes," he replied, "that is obvious; but why do they not execute the law? I observe that other papers characterize the article in question as purely sensational, and utterly without foundation, in fact."

"I see it all; I know it all now," I exclaimed; for, as a flash of lightning, did the whole dawn on my understanding. The law had been put in force that night, and we had seen some of the victims. Instantly my spirit was *en rapport* with the whole machinery and its operation. The mayor of the city of New York was a lady; the Common Council was largely composed of ladies; the Board of Aldermen was no more, for it was Alder*women* now; and in the city detective service the ability of women to *keep* secrets as well as to find them out had been extensively tested. This first descent had been planned for some days, but even the press had been kept ignorant of the proposed measure, with the exception above mentioned. Tonight the police had pounced on the *sinners,* and not, as of yore, the sinned *against* – and the surprise was complete. What a simpleton I had been to rush to the police when I saw Mr. Stiggins in their custody, I thought; but, then, why be ashamed of a good impulse?

From police station to police station, all over the city, I seemed to go without the fatigue usually attendant on locomotion. What sights I beheld, and what sound I heard! Coaxing and bribery of policemen were attempted without result; cursing, swearing and threatening were equally futile. The law enacted that the name of every man thus taken should be advertised in the newspapers of the town, city or county in which the arrests should be made; also, that a large black-board should be hung daily on the outside of every police station, whereon should be conspicuously recorded the names of the culprits brought to such station. This, I saw, was the lash that cut them, in anticipation of which the majority whined like whipped curs.

One stout, handsome gentleman, with his hands in his pockets, and looking up from a sort of brown study, seemingly of the floor or of his book, but really of his situation, said: "Well, gentlemen, we are finely sold; it is an unpleasant piece of business; d — d smart, women's wits have outwitted us, every one; that paper was right, if the others did call it sensational; *Woodhull & Claflin's Weekly* was right; it took women to keep it quiet and women to find it out; diamond cut diamond. I wonder how many and who of us will be sent to those houses for the reformation of prostitute men?"

The majority of his hearers laughed, but were nevertheless greatly perplexed and annoyed. "Just think," he continued, "of our names being in every paper to-morrow morning! Oh ye gods and little fishes! Our wives, our lady loves, our families! Think, gentlemen, of the long list of names that will to-morrow ornament every police station! Show yourselves appreciative of the loving kindness of the corporation in supplying us with so large an amount of gratuitous advertising! Perhaps for a trifling fee they would also allow us to exhibit our business cards on the black-board, in juxtaposition with our respective names. We are in for it, gentlemen, and no mistake, and seeing we must advertise, willy nilly, let us get all we can for the money; we can, after all, make this thing pay if we work it right."

"Confound the women!" exclaimed an old grey-headed gentleman who was standing on the right hand of the speaker; "we might have known how it would be if ever the women got the law into their own hands."

"I beg the gentleman's pardon," said a third gentleman, "But I don't see how we could have known that women would have turned the tables on us so nicely; but I suppose it is all right; we have got free so far, while the poor women were made to suffer all the shame and disgrace; to-night we have chanced to see how we like it."

"That is so with a vengeance," said another. "Yes, we are caught in a fine trap," exclaimed a fifth.

In one station-house seventeen gentlemen had just arrived, one of whom was bitterly denouncing petticoat government. "We were fools ever to give the wretches any power; finely are we paid off for our chivalry!"

"It seems to me," said a young fellow on whose face was a reckless, don't-care expression, "that to-night, against our wills, we are made to *act* a little of our chivalry." Some laughed aloud, but more imprecated interiorly. Then the voice I first heard of the seventeen resumed: "Here we are to-night, looking like a set of whipped curs. Oh, the cunning, crafty women! I tell you, gentlemen, a woman in craft equals the old gentleman below with horns and hoofs. See how astutely they have worked the machine – the law a dead letter until to-day, as we confidingly trusted that it would so remain; then, as in a steel trap, we are secured in its iron grasp. Oh, nothing can equal a woman! Serves us right, gentlemen, for giving them power."

Some cursed and swore for very madness, while others said they did not care, as their names were of no consequence. "But," remarked another, "perhaps the houses for the reformation of male prostitutes may be of consequence," shrugging his shoulders suggestively.

Then again in my dream there was a chasm of time not bridged over, either by events or memory. It was morning – early morning – and the newsboys were calling out, "The Prostitute Act enforced!

one thousand arrests!" They reaped, as might well be supposed, a most liberal harvest. What crowds gathered around the police station to read the names! There came to me at that moment not only the power to float from house to house, from building to building, but a sort of omnipresence that enabled me to see the whole effect of the late movement, and what, in that respect, was being said and done in every part of the city.

At one station I was amused to hear a man with a deep, strong voice calling out the names as he read them from the blackboard for the edification of the crowd. Occasionally a name was greeted with a general laugh or exclamation of surprise; while, as I passed through the crowd, I heard – or, shall I say, *saw?* – exclamations unuttered, such as, "Is it possible?" *"That* name!" "Astonishing!" "Surprising!" etc., etc. Around the newspaper offices were such large crowds that to keep order the policemen placed them in a double file. Those in the rear or outside would frequently offer large prices for the place of some one in front, so as to make sure of the coveted intelligence and avoid delay, the presses being quite unable to keep pace with the unusual demand. All were eager to see the names of the suddenly famous one thousand, and the telegraph operator had been busy ever since two in the morning transmitting names and other particulars of the enforcement of the law.

I beheld, too, the astonishment of heads of families when the morning paper was looked over, and headings like these met the eye:

THE PROSTITUTE ACT ENFORCED!
OVER ONE THOUSAND ARRESTS!
Preachers and Publicans, Pharisees and Pugilists,
DIVES AND LAZARUS,
All in a heap!!!
SAINTS AND SINNERS, SENATORS AND SLOP SELLERS!!!!
"Black spirits and white-blue spirits and gray,
Mingle, mangle, mingle, ye that mingle may!"
And now there's the devil to pay!!

I perceived, too, in the minds of almost every one, men as well as women, the *justice* of the proceeding was recognized. "It needed woman to administer justice," I heard a gentleman say to his wife at the breakfast table; "the late act," he continued, "has attracted the attention of thousands of earnest and influential people to this subject who have never before seriously thought on it. These poor women were liable at any time to be pounced on by policemen, dragged to the station house, sent to prison, or houses of reformation, perhaps heavily fined, and there was no one to help them or save them from disgrace. To avoid these arrests they were compelled to bribe the police and others, to pay very high prices for board, in order to compensate those who boarded them for the risk incurred of police descents, etc. To meet these enhanced expenses and avoid arrest, these women were compelled to prostitute themselves far more, and sink into deeper degradation. Thus the practical working of the law tended to greatly increase the evil, while its real supporters – the men – were scarcely ever molested."

"Poor things!" said the wife – oh, so tenderly! "and perhaps the majority of them were led into their life of shame because corrupt men caused their ruin in the first place."

This dream of mine includes such a long period of time, so great a variety of incident, and has already taken so much space for its narration, that I must hasten to the close. Imagination must fill up the scenes enacted in the courtrooms to which the prisoners were brought for examination and disposal. There was no sham about it – no half-way measures, the character and history of each prisoner was thoroughly investigated, and those proved to be habitually licentious were duly sent to the houses of reformation for such characters. Into these houses woman's shrewdness and good sense had entered, for they were not prisons, nor were their inmates told that they were lost, degraded, sinful, polluted beings, but they were instructed in physiology – in the consequences of use and abuse of every organ of the body, on the holiness of love and sanctification of the coming together of the sexes when legitimatized by holy and god-like motives. In my dream I visited four of those houses, which had been built and furnished at public expense. They were, in deed and truth, *Houses of Reformation*, and their inmates were treated as diseased patients not as miserable sinners.

Then my spirit realized how much more efficient for good, in this instance, had been woman's wisdom than man's much-boasted intellect; and while thus thinking, thinking, thinking how woman had cut the Gordian knot of the social evil – the knot which man feared even to touch – I awoke, and, to my astonishment, found it was all a dream; that we had no woman President, no woman legislators, and that the "*Social evil*" remained, as heretofore, the great moral ulcer of the nineteenth century; that the very laws enacted under a pretence of suppressing it were really aggravating its worst evils, inflicting the greatest curse on man in the very act of perpetrating the greatest injustice on unfortunate and defenceless women. And I said, would that our our legislators had the wisdom thus to grapple with the vexed question, or our women the power, as they had in my dream, to strike at the root of the evil by shielding the victim and enlightening the wrong doer!

Dream Number Nine.

IF a woman grow a cabbage and take it to the market, she sells it for just as much money as would a man had he grown the cabbage.

This I said to myself as I passed through the market yesterday and saw a woman selling cabbages. I bought one of her for fifteen cents. "Are you from the country?" I asked.

"Yes, indeed," she replied pleasantly. "I am a widow, but I have a nice garden spot where I grow my cabbages, potatoes and other things for market."

"You spade your garden, plant your seed and do all the work yourself?"

"Yes, indeed."

"Have you children?"

"I have two little fellows, but they are not old enough to help me any."

"You are a farmer, then, eh?"

"Not exactly," she replied, laughing; "but I have two cows; I have customers for my butter here in the city; then I have an apple orchard — only a little one. I have rented just now three acres of land near my place; so next year I will have potatoes – a good many – to sell."

"And," I said, "you will sell your vegetables for just as much money as would a man?"

"Oh, yes," she replied.

"And so you have *Woman's Rights*?"

"That is so, that is so!" she said with a laugh; "yes, yes! Woman's Rights!"

I walked away meditating; I meditated all the way home, and now I have had a dream which I believe was the result of that woman, her cabbages and my meditations thereupon. I am compelled, however, to confess that this dream which I am about to relate was not given to me in the night-time. It came to pass that when I arrived at home with my cabbage and marketing, I was so tired and sleepy that I laid down on the sofa in the parlor and went sound asleep. Yes, I have slept three hours; have just woke, and must now make haste and write my dream before my husband comes home from the office.

I dreamed that I was flying – or rather floating – through the air. Is it not a delightful feeling? How happy it makes one feel to dream of flying! Well, it seemed to me that I was high in the air and moving rapidly. Hamlets, villages, towns and cities, also the vast expanse of field, meadow, wood, river and lake were spread out as a map to my delighted gaze. But oh, the smoking, dirty cities! As I passed over them something drew me to descend, not that I so desired, but that the collective magnetic forces of the human beings therein immured, deprived me not only of the power, but, in a great degree, of the disposition to resist. So I came near enough to the surface to view the dark alleys, the narrow streets, the dark, brick walls of houses huddled together, and I longed to fly from them and again behold the beautiful country; but I was compelled to linger in each city and visit hundreds of places of which I had heard but had never seen – every garret, cellar, workshop or workroom in which poor half-paid working women toiled. But I found very few, indeed, of such individuals. What could this mean? Then millinery stores, fancy stores and all other stores were visited; but the number of women employed was really very small and those few had not that pallid, under-paid, over-worked look usually characteristic of women in such positions.

Mystery of mysteries! I said to myself; who does all the slop-work of those great cities? Who make the shirts, drawers, etc.? Who does the tailor-work we have heard so much about women doing for a mere pittance? Then with a rapidity much greater than that of flying I seemed to visit the homes and places of business of those who did that work; but lo, it was principally done by men and boys! There were women, certainly; but few – very few – compared with the number which I supposed were employed on such work. What has become of the women? I asked myself. Has the race of woman tailors died out? Are they all married, and so have husbands to provide for them? No answer came. So into hotels, jewelry stores, telegraph offices, paint shops, where I knew that the advocates of woman's rights should be almost exclusively employed, I looked but found scarcely any women there. Into counting-houses, broker's offices and banks I looked; and though in these latter I found some women looking quite vigorous and contented, women were by no means in the majority.

Well, Perhaps they had all gone into "law, physic and divinity!" So, after considerable search, I found a few doctors' and lawyers' offices scattered here and there; but the occupation of that class of people seemed to be gone to a considerable extent – there were not one-tenth the number I expected to find; but about half the lawyers, and three-fourths of the few doctors remaining, were women. As to the pulpit, I couldn't exactly understand it, for many of the churches had been turned into lecture rooms; others had been fitted up as unitary homes; some had become polytechnic institutions and schools of science; and many of the tall steeples were transformed into observatories for the people. In about half of the churches, however, preachers were grinding away as usual, and about one-fourth of these were women.

It rejoiced me greatly to find banks wholly conducted by women, who were also, to a large extent, proprietors of stores, and seemed not to be excluded from any occupation. Still, the majority of business people were men; it was evident that but a small proportion of women were employed in business, and that the number of persons employed in what are called the professions was so few that the disappearance of women from so many employments could not be accounted for in that way. What had become of the great surplus population of poor working women? Was it possible that their work had been taken from them and given to the men and boys who seemed to fill their places?

Then sorrow came into my soul, and I said, "Alas, alas! it would seem that tens of thousands of women must be out of employment

– must be starving – who did manage to live, if ever so poorly, by the labor of their hand; at least seventy-five or ninety per cent of these women must be starving!" Then I remembered a book entitled "Apocatastasis," or Progress backwards. How I had laughed at the idea of progress backwards! But did not his look very much like "Apocatastasis?"

It would take too much space to detail all my wanderings through that and many other cities all over the Continent. It will be sufficient to state that from Maine to Texas, and from Florida to Alaska, what is now woman's usual work in cities was nearly all done by men. Had to women all become wealthy? It was evident that they had not taken all the lucrative employments once monopolized by men.

Then the scene changed, and I found myself walking along the sidewalk of that city, like other mortals. I was pondering on what I had learned, and was feeling very sad. By-and-by I lifted my eyes which, in my gloom, had been cast on the sidewalk, and lo, in every direction, large bills met my eye, headed with the words, "Fifty years ago!" "Semicentenarian festival!" Across the street were large banners, as we see on election days, in commemoration of some great event. On these were the same words, with appropriate emblems and devices. Flags of all sizes were hung out of the windows, and carried by little boys and girls in the streets, all having the same or similar mottoes. On one of these large banners was represented, on the left, a sickly, starving woman, sewing and shivering in a garret; beside her was a coffin containing a dead infant, the pointers of the clock indicated midnight. Under this were the words, "Fifty years ago!" On the right of the same banner were represented groups of beautiful, healthy, intelligent women and children, gathering fruit and flowers in the bright sunlight. This picture was entitled "To-day."

Most of the banners and flags were graced by the faces of two noble, earnest, beautiful ladies; but no names were given and only the words "Fifty years ago!" replied to my many questions as to the meaning. The bells rang joyously, and bands of music were in almost every street, but neither drum nor cannon brought back memories of war. The beautiful, the joyous and the free were manifested in every countenance. Maidens and matrons, boys and girls, gentle men and intelligent women, all participated in this celebration. But I could not learn from any of them what was its meaning, all seemed so fully occupied with their destination.

By-and-by the street cars came along, fluttering all over with small flags, on which were these same words, "Fifty years ago!" The cars were labelled, "For the Festival!" Then rattled along the street two carriages in which were seen the beaming faces of ladies and gentlemen, and smiling children, and flags fluttering, with the same words, "Fifty years ago!"

Slowly, patiently, with the crowed of pedestrians, I moved along in the same direction as the carriages and cars, which frequently passed me, decked out with those magic words. All at once I found myself approaching a magnificent pavilion, large enough to hold tens of thousands of people. What large and beautiful flags were unfurled to the breeze! Leaves and flowers were everywhere made to repeat, in wreaths, those predominant words, and it seemed as if the very atmosphere multiplied and repeated, in each constituent action, the words, "Fifty years ago!"

I entered the pavilion and beheld a sight, which, for beauty and magnificence, I never saw equalled. Never, while life may last, shall I forget this part of my dream. Verily, it was a paradise far surpassing any that Adam and Eve ever beheld. Here was gathered all the beauty belonging to the vegetable kingdom. Here fruits, flowers, spreading branches and crossing vines were woven into a thousand floral arches over our heads – formed into summer bowers, grottoes, shady walks, secluded retreats. There were miniature lakes, waterfalls, fountains, fish ponds that surprised and delighted my eyes. Here were gathered specimens of all flowers, edible fruits, grains and vegetables grown in the United States. Ladies – only ladies – presided over all this wealth of beauty. Then I looked up and beheld in letters of living flowers and vines these words:

Women's Agricultural Fair.

I looked at the beautifully-executed design, and many times repeated to myself the words, "Women's Agricultural Fair."

"This is a most beautiful place," I remarked to an old gentleman who was leaning on his staff, looking up and about him, evidently feasting his eyes.

"Yes, grand, grand!" observed the old man.

"Will you inform me," I asked, "what is the meaning of this festival, or how it originated?"

He appeared astonished at my question, but soon showed by his countenance that he had decided me to be in earnest.

"You are a stranger, I see," he replied. "well, this is called the 'Women's Agricultural Fair' because everything you behold here – no matter what – has been grown by women agriculturists. It is this year combined with a semicentennial festival for the following reasons: Fifty years ago, a large surplus population of poor, toiling women, crowded our cities, while the land was not one quarter cultivated, causing, on the one hand, high prices for provisions, and, on the other, low prices for labor. "From him that hath not shall be taken away even that which he hath." To-day that large class of women who have no family duties and no husbands to provide for them are in the country; and they are no longer poor but are saving money. Besides these unmarried women and widows there are large numbers of married women in the country, many of them with families, carrying on farms, their husbands remaining in the city for a few years in order to get money to pay for and improve their farms and furnish their homes with requisites for comfort, culture, and refinement. In this way our cities are but little overstocked either by workingmen or workingwomen; for just as soon as their farms are paid for and sufficiently improved, the men, too, go to their farms and remain there."

Before us played a fountain of water in the center of a miniature lake, in the depths of which beautiful salmon sported, and on its surface water-fowl were swimming and diving. From its banks were reflected orange and fig trees, lemon trees and grape vines, all laden with fruit, and kindly shading the old man as he sat in a rustic chair.

"Take a seat," he said, pointing to one near him; "take a seat. We may as well rest while we talk." How, at this moment I recall that spot! What beauty, what wide spreading branches, what luscious fruit hung all about us!

"Now," said the old man, as he rested his two hands on his stick, "let me tell you how all this has come to pass."

"I would like it, if you please."

"Fifty years ago to-day the first Womans' Agricultural Convention was held. The call was made by two brave, beautiful women, who had made a business of Agriculture for ten years. There are their portraits," he said, as he pointed with his stick through an avenue of trees, "by-and-by you can go and take a near view; they will bear close criticism; one of them has passed to the farther shore, but the other is still in the physical body. Ah, you ought to see her! She is very old, but beautiful, so beautiful! She seems to have absorbed into herself the essence of the fruits and flowers and natural beauties which she so devotedly loves. Her eyes are blue and her face beams with goodness and intelligence. She can make a speech as well as ever, though she is now eighty-seven years of age. Well, these two ladies, as I said, had made agriculture a business for ten years. Having tested the matter to their own satisfaction, they resolved to urge others, particularly women, to adopt the same business. Every winter both of them left their farms, for a month or two, to lecture on *Agriculture For Woman*. Thus others joined them, and in a few years numbers of women had secured land for themselves and had engaged in its culture to great advantage.

"To make a long story short, it came to pass that just fifty years ago to-day the first *Womans' Agricultural Convention* was held. I was there. The best hall in the city was secured, and there was a large attendance. Many women were on the platform who owned their farms and houses, and they really made some excellent speeches, abounding with eloquence and logic, for they were both experienced and earnest in their plans for redeeming woman from poverty and privation.

"How well I remember some of the ideas advanced by one of them. 'We tillers of the soil,' she said, 'have discovered the great royal road to wealth — wealth and independence for woman. On this platform are thirty-five ladies who have demonstrated in their own lives that agriculture is woman's work just as much as it is man's work. Those ladies own farms and houses, cows and horses, of their own'; then, turning round, 'and I believe every one of you has money in the bank. You are healthy, you are happy, and this has been done not in your miserable cities, not in garrets, not for cheating slop shops, but by each person in independence.' How she did urge poor working women to go into the country if they only had just enough to take them there! 'Farming,' she continued, 'with the machinery now at command, is far easier and lighter than it was when we were children, and it is only habit and tradition that causes it to be regarded as requiring great muscular power. In general, it is much easier work, and far less exhaustive, than cooking, washing, ironing or sewing, especially in view of the accompaniments of fresh air and abundant food, in the one case, contrasted with foul air and semi-starvation in the other. At any rate, if it is not easier, we can do it, as it pays better and fills our pockets; and money is a great stimulant, as well as country air, beautiful scenery, fruits, flowers and singing birds.'

"I really believe I could remember most of her speech. However, she continued by informing the audience that she had purchased a large tract of land, on which she could immediately employ twenty-five women, and hoped that number would volunteer to go, as she would pay them more wages than they could earn at any sort of sewing until they could purchase some of her land themselves, after which she would rent to them, at a low price, various farming machinery, so that they could work to the utmost advantage. Fifty-seven volunteered at once; twenty-five were selected, all of whom succeeded – a wonderful success, I think. The callers of the Convention were so encouraged that more were held in various parts of the country, and the movement rapidly grew into a power, and its adherents were numbered by hundreds of thousands. All did not go into heavy farming; many concentrated on grain culture, as machinery enabled them to perform most of the labor with ease; many made a specialty of fruit; some of poultry, and others grew rapidly rich by pisciculture. Some settled in southern California, cultivating oranges, lemons, nuts, grapes, peaches, etc., or raising silkworms, while others profitably raised berries in the immediate vicinity of large cities. Finely they were caricatured by reckless, half-starved, half-intoxicated 'Bohemians,' always ready to sell their birthright of brains for a very small mess of pottage, and too lazy to work at any useful calling! Editorial wiseacres wrote labored articles to prove the utter futility and demoralizing tendency of any attempt by women to live by cultivating the soil. The popular lecturer said that a woman might as well attempt to keep a livery stable or a bowling alley, or pre-empt 160 acres of land in the moon, as to try to carry on farming; that, by attempting it, women would become rough, uncouth and masculine, and no man, who loved refinement and delicacy in woman, would ever marry such, etc., etc., etc.

"I have two sisters who were left widows when quite young; both with children. After the deaths of their husbands they came home to father's house. One had a little over a thousand and the other but three or four hundred dollars. After many long talks as to what was best to be done (for it was really a serious question with so many children), they finally purchased for a thousand dollars ten acres of land, on which was a small house; they planted trees, or rather paid a man to plant their fruit trees, and then went to work to raise vegetables for the city market. Their children became, every year, more and more useful. In ten years their success was complete; they had a fine orchard of choice fruit, a comfortable house and commodious family carriage, their boys are grown, and all of them farmers. My sisters taught the girls the importance of being self-sustaining, paid them for all work done by them in the garden or orchard, and at twenty each girl owned a piece of land. One of them, however, is now in the city with her husband, and together they carry on a large mercantile business. But," he remarked, "I am afraid I shall tire you; old age, it is said, tends to induce garrulity."

"Not at all; I am glad to hear you," I replied.

"Oh, it amused me," he continued, "to see how the women have stolen a march on the men. Yes, yes, they have outwitted them. You see we have a numerous race of dandies and would be do nothings who prefer a good fit, morocco shoes, gloved hands, sidewalks and high brick houses to anything else in the world. This race of men had fashionable mothers and equally silly fathers, as thousands of children have to-day, who are taught by their fathers and mothers that the preceding requisites are indispensable to respectability."

"Yes," I rejoined, "and I am thinking of the little boys of whom mothers are saying to-day, 'Willie or Johnny is going to be a lawyer, a doctor, or a preacher or a fine gentleman, or he is going into business (meaning the business of trying all the time to outwit somebody else, and persuade somebody to put money in his pocket without an equivalent.)"

"Yes," replied the old man, "and thus the supply of would-be do nothings exceeds the demand, and hence the surplus of empty-headed, little-brained dandies afraid of any business that would bring them within the class of mechanics. These, by the pressure of want, are necessitated to fill the places once filled, but now vacated, by the very women who are now far removed from cities, from poverty and from toil, with the birds, the flowers, the trees and the beautiful of which they are a part; and those shams of men fill their places in garrets and cellars."

"Nature has taken her children to her home and heart," I remarked.

"Just so, my friend," he replied; "birds, flowers, hills, rivers, mountains, running brooks and women should never be separated. There is," he continued, "a feature of this Agriculture for women that I should mention; it is this: You probably know that in all our large cities we had a super-abundance of honest mechanics. These, having seen what women could do in the country, concluded to try what *men* could do. The experiment succeeded to that extent that the only surplus populations in our large cities to-day are the miserable weaklings I have before mentioned as having fashionable mothers, who have little ability and less disposition to perform useful labor."

Then I thought in my dream that I arose to leave, and, shaking hands with the old man, thanked him for the pleasure his conversation had afforded; then directed my steps to the portraits of the two noble women who were the first to originate any extensive movement for placing women on the land. My whole being throbbed with happiness as I walked through the long avenue of trees, trails and flowers and noted the hundreds of healthy, happy women who presided over the specimens of their own culture. verily, woman has worked out her own salvation! I said to myself; the good time coming has surely come; woman has planted herself on the soil. She has health, she has wealth, and with these she has power. Self-salvation – this is the rock on which she has built; and not all the powers of hell shall prevail against it.

Then I found myself in front of the two portraits which the old gentleman had pointed out to me. While admiring them he came and introduced me to the surviving original, a dear old lady, whose hand I grasped with feelings akin to devotion. With her hand yet grasped in mine I awoke. A dream! I said in astonishment; but may not this dream, after all, be a prophecy?

www.ingramcontent.com/pod-product-compliance
Lightning Source LLC
Chambersburg PA
CBHW070214290526
45789CB00002B/985